MODERN MEDIA IN THE HOME

An Ethnographic Study

MODERN MEDIA IN THE HOME

An Ethnographic Study

Hugh Mackay and Darren Ivey

John Libbey - CIC Publishing

British Library Cataloguing in Publication Data

Mackay, Hugh, 1952–
  Modern media in the home: an ethnographic study
  1. Community   2. Mass media – Wales
  I. Title   II. Ivey, Darren

  307'.09429
  ISBN: 1 86020 598 4 (Paperback)

Published by
John Libbey Publishing - CIC srl, Corso Trieste 42, 00198 Rome, Italy
john.libbey@libertysurf.fr; www.johnlibbey.com

Orders (outside US): Book Representation & Distribution Ltd: info@bookreps.com
Orders (US): Independent Publishers Group: frontdesk@ipgbook.com; www.ipgbook.com

Printed in Malaysia by Vivar Printing Sdn Bhd, 48000 Rawang, Selangor Darul Ehsan.

Contents

Acknowledgements

We should like to acknowledge and thank the following bodies that provided the funding for the research project that is reported in this monograph: The Open University's National Everyday Cultures Project, BBC Wales, Sianel Pedwar Cymru (S4C), Trinity Mirror and The Western Mail.

Carys Evans at S4C, June François at The Western Mail, Paul Godfrey at Trinity Mirror and Eilir Jones at BBC Wales worked closely with us as members of the project's steering group. We should like to thank them for their support and encouragement, as well as their consistently perceptive comments on our research and findings. Tony Bennett's support for the project, particularly around the time of its inception, has been appreciated; and Kevin Williams, doyen analyst of the media in Wales, has been an important source of ideas that have helped us to make sense of our data.

Papers based on the project were presented at two conferences and a seminar – the 'New Media and Old Media. The Impact of the Internet on the Mass Media' conference, Tromso, 2002; the European Association for the Study of Science and Technology conference, York, 2002; and a seminar at the School of Journalism, Media and Cultural Studies, Cardiff University, 2003. We should like to thank those who engaged in the sometimes lively debate that ensued for their contributions to these sessions.

The research depended on the remarkable co-operation of ten households in Wales. Darren Ivey spent an average of 26 hours with each household – calling in, talking, reading their newspapers, eating meals, watching television, and staying overnight with several of them. We should like to acknowledge their tremendous toleration and hospitality, and to thank them for putting up with us and for coping with our researcher for so long, often when all they wanted to do was to read the newspaper or watch the television.

Hugh Mackay and Darren Ivey

Chapter 1

Introduction

T his monograph reports a small-scale ethnographic research project that explored the uses of the breadth of the mass media in ten households in Wales in 2001–2002. It is very much a data-led study, one that connects the empirical data from these ten households to the key issues, concepts and theories in the literature. In this Introduction we raise some core ideas from debates on media users – though our aim is not to provide a comprehensive review of the literature and debates on media consumption.[1] In subsequent chapters we present our research findings, our ethnographic data, in the context of these debates, occasionally referring to theories and concepts from the literature, especially where we feel that readers may want to read further.

Ours is an empirical contribution with three particular qualities. First, it provides an *up-to-date* account of media in the home – of media use in the multi-channel, Internet era. One remarkably striking thing about the literature on media users is that most of it is about terrestrial-only days, with the VCR identified by some as offering the potential for dramatic transformation. We report how newer media technologies have changed this picture profoundly. Second, our work is unusual in that it addresses the *breadth* of mass media in the home. Another striking point about the literature on media users is that the press, radio, television and the Internet are each examined in what are almost separate paradigms, with little consideration of how the various media are interleaved, and with little cross-fertilisation of ideas in the study of the various mass media.

1   For this, readers may like to consult David Morley or Shaun Moores. See D. Morley (1992) *Television Audiences and Cultural Studies*, London, Routledge; or S. Moores (1993) *Interpreting Audiences*, London, Sage.

By examining a broad range of media in households, charting use across the breadth of the mass media, we are addressing the practical realities of convergence, and making a modest contribution to connecting these different strands of research. Third, our study focuses on *transformations*, the changes that are taking place in the contemporary media landscape. While it explores new and old mass media, it focuses in particular on the changes that are underway, on how older media are being transformed and how new media are being adopted.

The present is a particularly interesting moment in terms of such media transformations. We have already mentioned the development of the multi-channel environment in the UK (where nearly half of all households now have cable or satellite television). The plethora of new channels (for example, the 'rolling' news on *News 24* or *CNN*) and services (for example, shopping or video-on-demand) in some ways enhances choice, and certainly constitutes a challenge to public service broadcasting.

The growth of channels has been accompanied by new systems of regulation (for example, the continuing relaxation of restrictions on ownership), new media forms (for example, 'reality' television) and a proliferation of information and communication technologies in the home (including wide-screen television, video-game players, mobile telephones, mini disc and DVD players, and PCs).

These changes are taking place concurrently with a significant broader social and cultural transformation. In society generally there has been, in recent years, a growth of a more individualistic culture, new boundaries between the private and the public, a stronger focus on lifestyles, and an increasing emphasis on the 'consumer' and consumption activities – at the expense of notions of 'citizens'.

Finally, it is worth mentioning the changing political environment. With the development of the EU, and the arrival of devolution in the UK and possibly even within England, we are seeing the emergence of a new set of political institutions and with them possibilities for new 'image spaces' and new 'imagined communities'. Our study is of media consumption in Wales, where we examined changing patterns of community, national and other spatially-based identities – empirically grounding the stimulating work of Kevin Robins on image spaces.[2]

Paddy Scannell and David Cardiff explain, in rich and fascinating detail, how the BBC enabled access to and participation in a national community, synchronising social experience, and was thus *the* core cultural institution involved in the construction of the British nation.[3] At the same time, as the official history of BBC

2   David Morley and Kevin Robins (1995) *Spaces of Identity. Global Media, Electronic Landscapes and Cultural Boundaries*, London, Routledge.

Wales explains, the BBC played a key role in constructing 'Wales' and in developing it as a nation.[4] Broadcasting has been a major focus of the activity of the builders of national culture in Wales – as is demonstrated by research on the cultural project of broadcasters in Wales.[5] This makes Wales an interesting site for exploring the mass media.

Wales is a diverse and fragmented nation, but the arrival of the National Assembly for Wales provides the strongest yet *raison d'être* for a Welsh mass media. At the present juncture in the devolution process, they have a crucial role to play in engendering and allowing access to debates, and providing information about, and analysis of, the development of policies and politics. They have an important contribution to make in relation to citizenship and democracy, and to the construction of modern Wales as a cultural, social and political entity. This has been recognised, in that it has been estimated that broadcasting in Wales has had a budget increase of about £20m. as a direct consequence of devolution.[6]

Although Wales is not the most distinctive minority nation in the UK, it is probably the one with the most interesting broadcasting environment – because of Sianel Pedwar Cymru (S4C), the Welsh fourth channel, and because of the standing and use of the Welsh language.

S4C began broadcasting in 1982, the result of a long and determined campaign for a Welsh-language television channel, and took over the Welsh-language broadcasting that had previously existed on BBC Wales and HTV. It has a specific public service cultural mission: to serve the Welsh community and particularly the Welsh language. It commissions but does not produce programmes, and has a budget of £81 million per annum from the Treasury, plus 10 hours of programming from the BBC that are funded from the licence fee. It also sells its own advertising. On analogue it broadcasts about 40 hours of Welsh-language programming each week, and it broadcasts about 75 per cent of Channel 4 (UK)'s output as well, at slightly different times from the Channel 4 schedule. S4C Digital broadcasts about 80 hours a week in the Welsh language (and no Channel 4 programmes), and S4C2 broadcasts the National Assembly of Wales. Each

---

3   Paddy Scannell and David Cardiff (1991) *A Social History of British Broadcasting. Volume One 1922–1939. Serving the Nation*, Oxford, Blackwell.

4   John Davies (1994) *Broadcasting and the BBC in Wales*, Cardiff, University of Wales Press.

5   David Bevan (1984) 'The mobilization of cultural minorities: the case of Sianel Pedwar Cymru', *Media, Culture and Society*, vol. 6, pp. 103–117.

6   Leighton Andrews (2004) 'Finding its voice – the National Assembly for Wales and broadcasting policy 1999–2003'. Paper presented at conference on Communications in Wales after the Communications Act, Aberystwyth, March.

week S4C reaches about 900,000 viewers, 200,000 of them outside Wales – an interesting development that is facilitated by the multi-channel, digital environment.

Bi- or multi-lingualism, although commonly seen in England as an archaic anomaly, is a normal feature of the modern world. With the growth in numbers of economic and political migrants, and of other transborder flows, bi- and multi-lingualism are becoming increasingly significant phenomena. Immigrant minority languages, though, are very different from territorially based linguistic minorities within nation states. As Ned Thomas explains: 'Immigrant minorities, while they may in some degree want cultural support in the home country from broadcasts in their own language, also aspire to some degree of assimilation, and their languages do not live or die by the treatment they get in the host country; there is always the home country.'[7] In its culture and media policies the EU has supported minority languages and, of course, the 'project' of Europe involves multi-lingualism. The EU cannot be integrated on the basis of a single language as was the case with nation states. For a language to survive in the contemporary era, it has to enjoy access to the mass media; and the mass media are crucial for 'normalising' use of the language. Moreover, as Thomas discusses so fluently, 'rarely do minorities escape a stereotyping that mixes romanticization and contempt', and today the mass media are crucial for challenging outsiders' views of minority life.[8] Wales, of course, is unusual as a minority language because it shares its space with the most powerful language in the world. Whatever the distinctiveness of Welsh, it is a version of bilingualism, which is something that is common throughout Europe and the rest of the world, although not in England.

In sum, our research took place at a particularly interesting moment in terms of new technological systems of communication,[9] an environment in a state of some flux, and in a part of the UK that has some distinct and interesting characteristics in terms of its politics and its mass media.

We are interested in grounding these broader transformations by examining everyday media use, providing a snapshot of this changing environment in ten households. The impact of these broader phenomena *is* shaped by the machinations of media conglomerates and state institutions but it is also the product of

---

7   Ned Thomas (1995) 'Linguistic minorities and the media' in Philip Lee (ed.) *The Democratization of Communication*, Cardiff, University of Wales Press, p. 176.

8   Ned Thomas (1995) 'Linguistic minorities and the media' in Philip Lee (ed.) *The Democratization of Communication*, Cardiff, University of Wales Press, p. 180

9   Raymond Williams (1974) *Television: Technology and Cultural Form*, London, Fontana.

the activities of ordinary people in their everyday lives and the ways in which these activities connect with the mass media.

The media industries refer to their users as readers, listeners, viewers or users. We tend to use the term 'users' in an attempt to avoid aligning ourselves with the notion of consumers (as used in the context, say, of pay-per-view) as opposed to citizens (the term more prevalent in discourses of public service broadcasting). Rather, we use it as a perhaps unattractive term that is shorthand for, and encompasses, readers (of the press), listeners (to radio), viewers (of television) and users (of the Internet). At the same time, our study is not in the 'uses and gratification' tradition – the approach to the study of media use that considers how they satisfy human needs, but sees these needs as individual, rather than socially embedded. Rather, we are interested in how people 'domesticate' or 'creatively appropriate' media in their homes.[10] Implicit in such notions is that the media text, and indeed media technologies, are not entirely fixed or determined, but are shaped in part by consumption practices.[11]

Television audiences are commonly conceived of as families. In 1990 James Lull wrote that '"watching television" is a family activity'.[12] David Morley, while acknowledging that the family is changing (from its traditional, nuclear form) sees it as 'the principal image which broadcasters (and government) hold of the domestic audience for television'[13] and cites the Annan Committee that stated that people watch television in a family group, so its regulation is a family issue. Roger Silverstone concurs, seeing the family as the context within which media consumption takes place – a social setting with conjugal, parental and sibling relationships.[14] While this may be true of regulatory discourses, 'households' seems a more appropriate empirical category, and one that is less ideologically charged. Not all of our households *were* families, so while family relations are the basis of the dynamics of many households, and hence of our understanding of viewing, in other households different phenomena have greater explanatory power – youth subcultures, for example. The plethora of media technologies in

10   Roger Silverstone (1994) *Media and Everyday Life*, London, Routledge; Andrew Feenberg (1999) *Questioning Technology*, London, Routledge.

11   The focus of much of Hugh Mackay's research has been on how users shape technology. See Hugh Mackay *et al.* (2000) 'Reconfiguring the user', *Social Studies of Science*, vol. 30, no. 5, pp. 737–757.

12   James Lull (1990) *Inside Family Viewing: Ethnographic Research on Television Audiences*, London, Routledge, p. 148.

13   David Morley (1992) *Television Audiences and Cultural Studies*, London, Routledge, p. 164

14   Roger Silverstone (1996) 'From audiences to consumers: the household and the consumption of communication and information technologies' in James Hay *et al.* (eds) *The Audience and its Landscape*, Boulder, CO, Westview Press.

the home today and the widespread ownership of multiple devices (notably radios and televisions) mean that much media consumption takes place individually or in small groups within households. Our concern is with how the media are implicated in fragmentation and integration in households.

Media users are important for policy-makers largely because of debates about media effects – on which evidence is inconclusive, in that effects vary and are context-dependent. So, like all research on media users, this study connects with debates about media influence, the consequences of the media for communities and societies. Media users are also vitally important to media organisations, being the main measure of performance and the basis on which they prosper or decay.

Media organisations routinely amass and access a vast array of data on the users of their products and, to a lesser extent, the everyday lives of these people. Over many years they have developed and refined their research methods, which are largely quantitative in nature. In recent years their quantitative research findings have been supplemented by qualitative data – mainly from open-ended questions in structured interviews and from focus groups. These various methods are used to generate increasingly sophisticated data, as media organisations seek to maintain or improve their understanding of their users – in a market that is becoming more complex and fragmented. As well as media fragmentation, the form of families and households in the UK and elsewhere in the western world is becoming more diverse, and there is a growing awareness on the part of media organisations of the complexity of the context of media consumption: domestic households.

By any measure, the media today are enormously significant in everyday life. ABC circulation figures for May 2003 show that 3.5 million copies of *The Sun* are sold daily, nearly 2 million of *The Daily Mirror*, and 0.85 million of *The Daily Star*. *The Daily Mail* sells 2.3 million each day and *The Express* 0.9 million. In the 'qualities' market, *The Daily Telegraph* sells 0.9 million, *The Times* 0.6 million, *The Financial Times* 0.4 million, *The Guardian* 0.4 million and *The Independent* 0.2 million. Readerships are very much higher – with about 2.5 people reading each copy of a national newspaper, and slightly more a local or regional newspaper. Turning to how long newspapers are read for, and to local newspapers, recent research found that a copy of *The Western Mail* (the south and west Wales provincial daily) is read for an average of 36 minutes, *The South Wales Echo* (Cardiff's evening daily) for 30 minutes, and *The Post* (Cardiff's freesheet) for 12 minutes.[15] 75 per cent listen to radio every day and

---

15   Western Mail and Echo (2000) *Wales National Readership Survey.*

90 per cent of all adults every week, for an average of 24 hours a week.[16] 81 per cent of people live in households with two or more television sets, and 57 per cent of eldest children have a set in their bedroom. 85 per cent watch television every day, and 60 per cent watch television for three hours a day or more. 84 per cent have teletext, with 36 per cent using it on every day or most days, and 52 per cent using it occasionally or hardly ever. 44 per cent have Internet access at home and, of these, 39 per cent report that they use it daily, with email the major use, followed closely by research or looking for information.[17] There are considerable variations in these data according to age, gender, ethnicity, region and social class.

Such numbers and proportions suggest that the media play a major role in people's lives – but tell us nothing about *how* they are used or their significance. Questionnaires, diaries, set meters, people meters and passive people readers provide a wealth of quantitative data, but fail to distinguish between levels of engagement with the medium; nor do they tell us anything about the forms of viewing (or not viewing) or the significance of such activity – there is an assumption that having the television switched on is the same as 'watching television', or that 'watching' is the same as 'paying attention'.[18] Most of the data is used to generate averages and to identify regularities and generalisable patterns – to identify and classify 'typical' reading, listening and viewing behaviour. The limits in such systems were demonstrated forcefully in December 2001–January 2002, when the Broadcasters' Audience Research Board (BARB) changed the make-up of its panel to reflect more accurately the characteristics of the population as a whole. It also increased the size of its panel by 15 per cent, largely to measure the viewing of minority channels more accurately. The outcome was remarkable. For example, among upmarket young men, comparing January 2002 with January 2001, the audience for Film Four was down 67 per cent, MTV was down 26 per cent, ITN News was up 148 per cent, E4 was up 465 per cent and Carlton was up 1165 per cent. Similarly for radio, strong criticisms have been voiced regarding Radio Joint Audience Research (RAJAR), the official radio audience measurement body in the UK. These criticisms escalated in the light of research in 2003 that found very different listening figures. RAJAR (at the time of writing) relies on diaries, while a researcher (GfK Marketing Services) commissioned by Kelvin MacKenzie's Wireless Group used electronic wrist-

---

16   Approximate RAJAR figures for Wales, 2003.

17   This data is based on an interview survey of 1,191 adults (age 16+) in 2002. It is reported in Independent Television Commission (ITC) (2003) *The Public's View 2002*, London, ITC.

18   David Morley (1992) *Television Audiences and Cultural Studies*, London, Routledge.

watches to record what listeners listen to. The disparities were huge, with RAJAR finding 10 million Radio 4 listeners and GfK finding 17.9 million Radio 4 listeners, and with RAJAR finding 13.2 million Radio 2 listeners and GfK finding 15.2 million Radio 2 listeners.[19] Anyway, RAJAR does not distinguish between different levels of attentiveness – a listener is simply someone who is within earshot of a radio for at least five minutes in any quarter of an hour. These are a couple of the ways in which we can see that audiences, or consumers, are far from an objective measurement.

Data on qualitative matters that is gathered by the media industries is in some cases extensive, but it tends to be quantitative. A recent questionnaire survey of 1,005 adults commissioned by *The Western Mail* included questions on readers' frame of mind when reading the newspaper (relaxed, looking for information, and so on); how they normally bought their copy; what they feel about Wales and Welshness; which sections of the newspaper (sport, local news, and so on) they are interested in; what other newspapers and magazines they read; what radio, television and teletext they listen to, view or access; and so on. While these questions are about what many would consider qualitative issues, the data gathered in this questionnaire made extensive use of 7-point scales, and is quantified. The main way in which qualitative data is gathered by media organisations is through focus groups – wherein a suitable sample of members of the public are assembled to answer and discuss questions. Typically, however, focus groups undertaken for media organisations involve note-taking and abbreviated summary, rather than the lengthier analysis that is associated with focus groups conducted by academics. Both forms of data collection, however, are 'second-hand', in that they are what people report, what they *say* that they do. Obviously, such accounts are likely to vary significantly from the activity undertaken in its real-life context. In the context of focus groups, the social dynamics of the group are likely to lead participants to modify or moderate their views and perceptions in the light of what other participants have said. While there are 'viewer appreciation indices', these are not a major element of broadcasters' knowledge of their users. So most qualitative data collected by the media industries is fairly limited or restricted in scope, in the context of a prevalence of quantitative data. Whether qualitative or quantitative, media users and the differences between them are described in terms of only a few, rather generalised, variables, with other aspects of identity and difference ignored. By contrast with most industry research, our interest is less with demographics and large popu-

---

19   'R4 to the fore – or is 2 still No 1?', *The Guardian*, 29 May 2003, p. 21.

lations, and more with the subjective experience of media use and the diversity of users.

Our research is concerned with getting behind the figures, the statistics and the averages, problematising the categories and unpicking the generalisations that obscure the specific aspects of particular settings in which the mass media are used. So it complements existing data and analysis – by investigating first-hand the context of consumption: media consumption does not take place in a vacuum, so we have explored how the media are used in context, and their significance for everyday life in households. Rather than objectifying media practices, we explore the complexities, the particularities and the idiosyncrasies. While Ien Ang argued in the 1990s that broadcasters were not interested in such data,[20] it is clear that today ethnography is a method in which media organisations have a growing interest – as a part of their never-ending quest to know their users better.

Our research explores media use by investigating everyday life in ten households. Details of our research methods, and our reflections on the fieldwork, are provided in the Research Methods Appendix. We spent an average of 26 hours with each household – talking with its members, undertaking semi-structured interviews, participating in a limited way in their everyday life, and observing their interaction. Material was recorded using fieldnotes (made during as well as after the fieldwork), audio and video tape recordings and a camera, and our research subjects completed a diary of their media consumption over a week. Drawing on this mass of data, we provide in this book the 'thick description'[21] that characterises ethnographic work.

The study follows closely the work of David Morley.[22] Morley builds on Stuart Hall's work on encoding and decoding, which focuses on how audiences make sense of media messages and is thus a more complex model of power than the one-way process implied by notions of media 'effects'.[23] Morley displaced the central position of the media text for understanding audiences, countering media-centrism and shifting the focus from the text to the *context*. One effect of this shift of focus is that we found much media use to be highly mundane. Like Morley, we have explored how media consumption is embedded in everyday life in households, how it intersects with domestic rhythms and routines. Our concern is with the broad and complex cultural, social, political and economic processes

20   Ien Ang (1991) *Desperately Seeking the Audience*, London, Routledge.

21   Clifford Geertz (1973) *The Interpretation of Cultures*, New York, Basic Books.

22   David Morley (1992) *Television, Audiences and Cultural Studies*, London, Routledge.

23   Stuart Hall (1973) 'Encoding and decoding in the television discourse', Stencilled Paper, University of Birmingham, Centre for Contemporary Cultural Studies.

in which media consumption is embedded – not abstracted individuals with simply personal needs, but people in the social setting of the domestic household, the context that shapes their interpretative practices. So our focus is on the context, the micro setting of media use, rather than on programmes or texts. In calling for a decentering of the television as the research focus, Morley and Silverstone argue that media consumption studies should extend to other information and communication technologies.[24] We have gone further to address the press and radio as well – providing a brief account of the full breadth of the mass media in the lives of the members of our ten households.

Having said that, like any researchers, at the outset we had to define some boundaries for our study – to decide what to include as context, and where it stops.[25] Not all media consumption takes place in the home – the physical base of household activity – but that has been our focus. For a full picture of media consumption we would have had to study leisure, community, and the whole of society. We have followed Morley on this (like him), aware that while addressing the context of consumption we have to be pragmatic about defining that context. Working in households was enough (and hard enough) for a project of this scale – but we recognise that the context of media consumption in reality extends beyond the home.

Having established a boundary for the research, and confined our attention to the home, our approach has been to gather data on the fine-grained detail of people's daily routines, and to record and analyse our data by focusing on how people felt and the significance, or meaning, of their activities. The significance of media use, for any one person, is context-dependent; it varies from one situation to another. We explore the dynamic interactions of household members with others both co-present and – in a mediated form – distant. Such interaction is shaped by power relations – which vary according to the part of the house and the time of day, as well as between household members. Media use intersects with the material and symbolic resources of households – what Silverstone refers to as their 'moral economy', on the grounds that members' economic activities are informed by a set of values and aesthetics that, in turn, are informed by history, biography and politics.[26] We examine the place of the media in people's

24   David Morley and Roger Silverstone (1990) 'Domestic communication: technologies and meanings', *Media, Culture & Society*, vol. 12, no. 1, pp. 31–55.

25   John Corner (1991) 'Meaning, genre and context: the problematics of "public knowledge" in the new audience studies' in J. Curran and M. Gurevitch (eds) *Mass Media and Society*, London, Edward Arnold.

26   Roger Silverstone, Eric Hirsch and David Morley (1992) 'Information and communication technologies and the moral economy of the household' in R. Silverstone and E. Hirsch (eds) *Consuming Technologies. Media and Information in Domestic Space*, London, Routledge.

day-to-day lives and social relationships – how the media are used and made sense of, and the sorts of experiences, interaction and identities that they sustain.

We have explored these phenomena and processes empirically in contemporary Wales. We have examined how the mass media provide (or are slotted into) a structure for the day and the week. We have considered ways in which they provide pleasure, distraction, fulfilment, engagement, information and confirmation.[27] We have addressed how they are used to facilitate the construction of personal space in the home, and how they bring people together while maintaining distance between them, connecting while apart, and mediating interaction. We have explored ways in which they transport people, metaphorically, to distant places and cultures, making connections with people, events and places that would otherwise remain unknown. We have addressed how they connect the private world of the home with the public world beyond, linking the domestic sphere with various 'imagined communities', and thus shaping a common culture. Finally, we have considered how, through interaction with and via the media, identities are expressed and constructed. In short, we have explored the role the media play in reflecting and reproducing, indeed constituting, social life.

Chapter 2 of this book provides an 'ethnographic portrait'[28] of each of our ten households. This provides a description of the context and nature of their media consumption, describing each household member, their lifestyle, domestic space, everyday routines, uses of the media and senses of Welsh identity. These brief accounts say something about each household's ensemble of goods, practices, cultural tastes and social positioning that reflects (and is used to construct) the identities of the household's members. We thus map in an abbreviated way the diverse patterns of taste in our ten households. In the various chapters and sections that follow we build on these cameos of each household, adding further data and analysis on each. By the end, the reader should have a reasonably elaborate account of the place of the media in the everyday life in our ten households.

Chapter 3 is organised around the various media. Sections examine the consumption of the press, radio, television and new media – by which we mean computer games, the Internet and email. Like Chapter 4, it makes extensive use of quotations from fieldwork diaries and the reported speech of members of our households, bringing the account 'to life'.

27   Sonia Livingstone (1999) 'New media, new audiences?' New Media and Society, vol. 1, no. 1, pp. 59–66.
28   Roger Silverstone and David Morley (1990) 'Families and their technologies: two ethnographic portraits' in Charles Newton and Tim Putnam (eds) Household Choices, London, Futures Publications.

Television audiences are studied by many disciplines, approaches and methods. In spanning the breadth of the mass media (their readers, listener and users, as well as television viewers), this range of perspectives becomes very much broader. In terms of qualitative studies of use, we find enormous differences in the research traditions of the various mass media. Television viewing is undoubtedly the most developed area – with ethnographic studies generally focusing on specific genres or programmes.[29] Radio audiences are less 'captivated', because the radio is commonly listened to in conjunction with some other activity, and is often listened to for lengthy time-spans that do not correspond with programmes, so studies of reception lead readily from text to context – though there is precious little research.[30] There is extraordinarily little research on the practices of newspaper reading,[31] and very few studies that span the full breadth of the mass media in everyday life. Our own attempt at gathering data across this breadth means, inevitably, that our study is relatively superficial in relation to any one mass medium.

The data we have gathered – like any data – has to be interpreted: the facts do not speak for themselves. In making sense of our data we have been informed and guided by the analyses of media consumption that previous academic researchers have developed; the interests of the media organisations involved in the project; and our own interests and intuitions. Reading and discussing the fieldnotes, we arrived at a set of questions or categories that emerged from our reading of the data. In Chapter 4, more than any other, we have combined our knowledge of academic debates about media consumption with our data. In Chapter 4 we organise our data in terms of what seem to us core issues about, or ways of making sense of, the domestic consumption of the mass media. We examine temporal rhythms, domestic space, gender, spaces of identification, and the Welsh language. In Chapter 4, on 'Temporal rhythms', we explore the temporal dimensions of domestic routines of media consumption, and the section on 'Domestic space', is concerned with the use of different parts of the home by different household members for the consumption of particular media. Gender

29 Although Janice Radway's work stands out because she advocates researching 'the kaleidoscope of daily life', rather than starting with a genre or medium. See J. Radway (1988) 'Reception study: ethnography and the problems of dispersed audiences and nomadic subjects', *Cultural Studies*, vol. 2, no. 3, pp. 359–376.

30 Andrew Crisell (1986) and David Hendy (2000) each have chapters that review research on listeners/audiences of radio. See A. Crisell (1986) *Understanding Radio*, London, Methuen; and D. Hendy (2000) *Radio in the Global Age*, Cambridge, Polity

31 The few exceptions include Mark Pursehouse's research on readers of *The Sun*. He found that readers identified with *The Sun's* light-hearted approach, puns, appeals to common sense, fun style and not taking life too seriously. See M. Pursehouse (1991) 'Looking at "*The Sun*": into the nineties with a tabloid and its readers', *Cultural Studies From Birmingham*, vol. 1, pp. 88–133.

is a crucial dimension of power or politics in the domestic sphere, so it is central for understanding the household dynamics that provide the framework for the context of media consumption. The section on 'Gender' in Chapter 4 explores technological and other dimensions of the gendered nature of media consumption. The section 'Spaces of identification' is concerned with how people identify with their media, but also the imagined communities that are enjoyed, accessed or constructed with and through the media – at local, Welsh, UK and global levels. Finally, the section 'The Welsh language' examines issues about the media in relation to both fluent speakers and learners, in Welsh-speaking, mixed language and English monoglot households, raising questions about the mass media and minority languages.

The book ends with a short Conclusion in which our main findings are drawn together. This is followed by the Research Methods Appendix, which details and discusses the methods used in this research, and provides our researcher's reflections on his fieldwork with each household.

Chapter 2

The households

W e begin by providing cameos of each of the ten households. Using pseudonyms and with a few other details changed, for reasons of confidentiality, these
'ethnographic portraits' outline some key aspects of the household: its members,
their occupations and ages; and their physical location, the nature of their
accommodation, its rooms, and how these are used. Each cameo says a little of
the history and lifestyle of household members, their work, income, activities
(together and separately), cultural tastes (and the ambience of their home), and
how they see themselves – their identities. We describe briefly the breadth of
media technologies in the household, where these are located, who they are used
by, when, how and for what purpose. We describe temporal and spatial aspects
of uses of the breadth of the mass media, identifying the various media forms
that are implicated in household members' daily lives. Finally, exploring spaces
of identification, we comment on our households' senses of Wales and Welsh
identity, and report their views of the Welsh language and the Welsh mass media.

Addey and Rowlands

Paul Addey and Christopher Rowlands share a two-bedroom rented flat above
a small convenience store in central Swansea. They each pay £35 a week in rent,
with most of Christopher's paid by Housing Benefit. The location of the flat near
to the city centre means that the lads have all their amenities and entertainment
within walking distance. Their flat acts as a base for their social activities, a
convenient place for friends to gather, or to return to, to continue the party. A
small living room is open-plan to a kitchen, and through this is the bathroom.

Access to the bedrooms is through the small and narrow living room. The flat is cluttered with dirty crockery, and a few guitars lie around.

Paul is 28, single, and works part-time as a day service office with the local authority's Social Services. He is about six foot three and his dress is very casual, an eclectic mix of student leather jacket and tracksuit, his hair generally unkempt, and he feels most comfortable in a pair of cream coloured loafers. Originally from the north of Swansea, Paul has lived in the city centre for five years, in shared houses and flats. He enjoys the occasional game of rugby and was following the British Lions tour to Australia when we began our fieldwork; he turns his newspaper straight to the sports page. He also takes kick-boxing lessons, but his main interest is performing as a guitarist in a local band. He spends most of his free time at his local pub, with his small and close-knit circle of friends – who all live within a two-mile radius. Paul is a Welsh learner who attends a night class and reads learner publications at home. He is now at quite a sophisticated level, with a very good grasp of the Welsh language. Paul is an English literature graduate of the University of Glamorgan.

Christopher is 27, also single, unemployed and getting occasional work as a session musician at the start of our research, but later working away as this career developed. He is a guitarist, like Paul, but wears more fashionable clothes than Paul does, the cheaper designer labels. He is an English-speaking monoglot, though he has a small vocabulary of Welsh from his school days. Christopher enjoys his time at home and is a keen Dreamcast player. He also loves *The Simpsons*, saying that he probably knows all the words to all of the episodes (a point proven when *The Simpsons* came on). Christopher also plays in a band, and several recording companies have expressed an interest in it. Towards the end of our research, Christopher was offered a contract as a session player with an artist signed to Sony Records, so started to work away for much of the time.

Until that time Paul and Christopher had both spent a lot of time at home because, they say, they could not afford to go out a great deal. Paul expends considerable effort cooking for himself, while watching television and listening to music. Occasionally Christopher's girlfriend Sam comes over, or Anna, who is both Paul's girlfriend and Christopher's sister. On such evenings, the first one home usually gets control of the entertainment in the living room and the comfortable chairs. Both occasionally leave the flat during the week to train at the local gym, or to rehearse with their respective bands at a local studio. For Paul this is more of a hobby or social event; for Christopher it is a serious attempt to get a record contract.

The flat has a small living room, with a wide-screen television and video, a DVD player and a CD stereo hi-fi system. Paul has a hi-fi in his room and a portable television. Christopher has a wide-screen television and video in his room, along with a hi-fi system. Christopher owns a Dreamcast games console that he keeps in the living room, while Paul owns a Sony PlayStation and a Super Nintendo 64. The living room is lined with a large selection of video games, music CDs and video cassettes. They subscribe to NTL World, which offers all the film and sport channels, and to an Internet service via the television set that they do not use because of problems with its reliability.

Paul buys *The Welsh Mirror* every day and *The Western Mail* occasionally during the international rugby season. Christopher tends not to buy a newspaper, but occasionally buys film and music magazines such as *Mojo* and *Empire*.

Christopher regularly listens to audio CDs, music videos and DVD films during the day. His daytime media consumption is usually spent alone, but he sometimes participates in group-viewing of sport with Paul or friends who call by. Paul, by contrast, uses the media more in conjunction with other activities such as cooking and eating. Both watch *The Simpsons* together on a regular basis and spend shared time in the living room during sports broadcasts and to share and compare new music purchases and finds. Paul's use of the media is patterned and regulated by his hours of work. The news features in his morning and evening routines, along with audio CDs and videos for entertainment. His use of the Welsh-language media is mainly educational, and his selection of digital programmes reflects his specialist music passion. Both Paul and Christopher tend to watch repeats of popular television shows shown on Paramount and UK Gold. Both enjoy video console games and have a selection of multi-player games that they occasionally use together. Christopher's media use focuses on audio and music videos, and he tends to watch MTV2. He spends most of his 'home' time in his own room. Paul spends considerable time alone, mostly in the living room, where the television and hi-fi provide the background to his relaxation. He occasionally retreats to the bedroom to read and to play video games late at night. However, the living room is used regularly by Paul to entertain friends with videos, console games and DVDs, often up to 1 a.m. during the week as well as at weekends. A console game, *Zelda*, was a semi-permanent fixture of the living room, available for play when wanted. They both said it was superb, and had other titles such as *House of the Dead* and *Wacky Racers*, which they play on the Dreamcast machine. This device usually comes out after the pub for whoever has come back to the flat, for some friendly competition. Paul and Christopher like to spend a lot of time in the flat: even on warm sunny days the games machine is switched on. Both mix and match their media, with frequent interchange during their time in the house, and their activities are centred on the living room. MTV is usually the staple when their friends are around because, as Paul said, it gives them a chance to "slag off other bands".

Domestic space is limited, and it was interesting to see who controls the living room and who is relegated to the bedroom. Paul dominates the living room area with his social activities and Christopher, with more media devices in his room, often retreats to his private space. The amount of electronic entertainment media concentrated in the small living space indicates that this room is a focal point for social get-togethers, a meeting place, an entertaining place, or somewhere to hang out. At one point Paul wanted to "get a place of his own" and said that Christopher was around the house too much – suggesting some conflict over space and the use of the entertainment devices in the small and cramped living room. For Paul the television and video in the living room – both rented – were his only source of entertainment; Christopher owns his own television and video which he keeps in his room. This seemed something of an annoyance for Paul. The dynamics of the control of space is one of the most interesting feature of this household: there seems to be a fine balance between 'together time' and 'private time'. Paul and Christopher seem to manage to prevent this becoming a major issue, perhaps through their game playing together and their shared taste in music and video. Although mostly fragmented in their use of the media and domestic space, they come together and use the living space to enjoy leisure activities together.

Paul is very concerned to learn the Welsh language, and to participate in what this will enable him to enjoy. He does not watch S4C on a regular basis, but watches the occasional programme to help his learning. He finds programmes without 888 subtitles too hard to follow, but the mix of Welsh and English on some programmes allows him to at least follow the plot. Paul thought that S4C Digital could be an opportunity to create a "learning zone" for Welsh learners at a regular time-slot, which would help him to break into the Welsh-language media. He said that S4C gave him a "look over the fence" at a different kind of Welsh culture. When pushed on this point, he said that he felt that he could see that there was a Welsh culture on display that he did not feel a part of, and that learning the language would in some way open this up for him. Paul had a conception of what was in the garden that appealed to his sense of Welshness, even though his understanding of its content was limited. This might suggest that the output of S4C creates a feeling that something is missing in his sense of his 'Welshness', which encourages him to learn the language. Asked if he thought he would feel 'more' Welsh if he could speak the language, Paul said that he feels "semi-Welsh" and does not feel a part of the 'Welshness' represented on S4C. His comments related to the programmes he had watched recently on S4C and S4C Digital – which included *Porc Peis Bach*; *Byd Natur*; *Ibiza, Ibiza, Ibiza*; and *Pobol y Cwm*. Although he feels outside the Welsh culture of S4C, Paul says that 'elitist' is too harsh a word to describe how he sees the culture it propagates; but he does not really feel he can identify with it, and in this respect it is divisive.

'Welshness' plays a major part in Paul's narrative of himself and seems to be a large factor in his desire to learn the Welsh language. The flat is adorned with a considerable quantity of Welsh symbolism – rugby shirts, flags, and large hats with dragons. It seems that rugby international days offer Paul the best chance of not simply looking over the fence but actually playing in the garden (to extend his metaphor). His wish to learn the language was a way of capturing the same kind of feeling that he experiences during internationals, the sense of identity that so far has seemed tantalisingly out of his grasp.

Chandler and Thomas

Stuart Chandler and Ann Thomas are both in their mid twenties and live together in a small two-up two-down flat on a terraced road in the middle of Carmarthen. They have lived in Carmarthen for six years, have lived together in the flat for two years, and work together at a government office in Carmarthen, where they are both administrative assistants. Their apartment is set off a terraced street, with room to park cars at the front, though neither of them owns a car – they walk to work, which is not far away. Stuart is the son of a minister from Ammanford, and Ann comes from Ystalefera, a Welsh-speaking part of the Swansea valley. Both Stuart and Ann are graduates in Humanities of Trinity College, Carmarthen. Both understand Welsh but are not fluent enough to be conversational. They see the town as predominately Welsh but also as cosmo-politan because of its student community.

Stuart is a well-built and tall, with long dark hair tied back in a pony tail which reaches the middle of his back. He is a rock and heavy metal fan, and wears a pewter pendant and some pewter rings on both hands. He is softly spoken and articulate, and is interested in playing the drums. He has formed a local band but they hardly ever have the chance to play, though they occasionally rehearse at Stuart's father's church hall near Ammanford. Stuart enjoys repeats of old sci-fi programmes and new shows such as the *X Files* and *Star Trek* spin-offs (for example, *Deep Space 9*). He tends to listen to his large and specialist collection of audio CDs rather than the radio, but also enjoys Radio Four discussion programmes.

Ann is in her mid-twenties, and dresses in a smart yet bohemian style, a designer hippy chick look. She wears new-age jewellery and very little make-up. Her tastes are rather different from Stuart's, so they spend considerable time using different media in different parts of the house. She watches television mostly upstairs, often soaps, while he enjoys Sky downstairs.

Their flat is clean and tidy. The décor is a contemporary floral design, which must have been the choice of the landlord. Both Stuart and Ann enjoy alternative music, and the living room has several racks of rock and heavy metal CDs. The walls are quite bare, with very little on display. An Indian dream-catcher hangs over the front window. The living room is quite cramped and gives few indications of their rock lifestyle. Although smart, the living room lacks a lived-in feel or any real expression of a personal style or theme. It is where they spend most of their time when at home – though they spend quite a lot time out socialising. The kitchen area is very small, so the living room is where they usually eat. The room is small and comfortable but quite dark, getting little sun because of its position. An open pine staircase leads upstairs, and there is a small kitchen at the back. This is well-equipped, with a small pine dining table, and through the kitchen window one can see a small garden which slopes upwards.

There is a small television and VCR in the corner of the living room. They pay £35 a month for Sky and see this as good value because of the extra sport and film packages. They have a Sony PlayStation and a portable television upstairs in their bedroom. This television receives a terrestrial signal only, and is watched mostly by Ann. They have two stereos with radios, one in their bedroom and the other in the living room.

There is a distinct lack of newspapers in the flat. Stuart usually brings the weekly *Carmarthen Journal* home from work; occasionally the daily *South Wales Evening Post* or *The Western Mail*, for the jobs sections. He prefers to read music magazines such as the weekly *Kerrang*, but is not heavily into news. Ann sometimes looks at the papers, if they are around, to scan the television guides, though she usually uses the Electronic Programme Guide (EPG). She sometimes buys *TV Quick* because there is no EPG upstairs. Stuart likes Sky television because it means there is always something that they can watch together. He says that if there is a conflict between them over programme choice, he can always watch the same show when it is repeated later the same day or later in the week. He is the one who, in a sense, occasionally sacrifices his preferences to

19

enable them to share space and time: Stuart watches what Ann wants and uses the VCR to record something to watch later. He values 24-hour programming and the repetition of programmes. Stuart shows us how more flexible media have intersected with household dynamics and challenged regimes of control, with greater fragmentation instead of time together. Greater choice has reduced conflict over the use of particular media technologies at particular times.

The couple's choice of programmes and radio is most distinctive. Stuart and Ann were keen to emphasise that multi-channel television gave them a chance to watch a better range of alternative music programmes and science fiction (for example, on the Kerrang! and Sci-Fi channels). They are regular followers of *EastEnders*, Ann in particular. Stuart also listens to Radio Four, though he said that he thought we might think that he was boring on this count. They seemed to recognise that their pattern of broadcasting consumption (popular programmes such as soap operas and radio talk shows) probably runs counter to the image they present through their dress.

Both liked Sky for its specialist music output and felt that digital offered them a greater choice in specialised programming– such as underground rock music. They said that S4C, BBC and HTV do not really cater for their tastes. They use terrestrial television mainly for local news, rather than buying a local newspaper. Nonetheless, they still think terrestrial television programmes and news are superior in quality to Sky. Discussing the relative popularity of channels in Wales, they saw S4C as different from the others because it does not seem to go for ratings but, rather, is content to cater for its specialist Welsh-language audience. Welsh content overrides a broader appeal and higher ratings. They felt that using English would introduce S4C programmes to a larger audience in Wales (referring to themselves as non-Welsh speakers). They saw BBC Wales as having a better output in terms of broad Welsh appeal, but criticised its programmes as clones of existing formula dramas and so on, albeit set in Wales. Even though these dramas are based in Wales, they do not have a particularly "Welsh stamp" – they are simply about "people who happen to live in Wales". They thought that, outside Wales, Welsh programming was perhaps seen as second rate. Stuart feels that "all the talented people move out of Wales".

Although they feel that the quality of television in Wales is good on the whole, they see HTV Wales and BBC Wales as having an important role to play in bridging the gap between S4C's restricted linguistic appeal and what they feel is the overriding "English feel" of Sky. They feel that Sky's main channel, Sky One, ignores Wales, but that S4C does not do any better in giving them a sense of 'Welshness'. BBC Wales and HTV could do a lot to bridge the gap by using the Welsh language in conjunction with their broader appeal, which might bring down existing linguistic barriers.

Stuart seems frustrated at losing his language skills. They both felt that after they left school, they lost the encouragement and motivation to keep up the language. He says that the National Assembly likes its workforce to speak Welsh but does not actively encourage them to learn Welsh during office time. Both Stuart and Ann wanted to see some integration of Welsh speakers and non-Welsh speakers in Wales, and saw changes in broadcasting practices – more bilingual programmes or programmes aimed at twenty-somethings that cross the linguistic barrier – as a way of achieving this.

Daniels

The Daniels' home sits on the brow of a hill overlooking Ammanford in Carmarthenshire. The house, built in the 1960s, has a large west-facing window with a great view of the town below and the Tywi valley in the distance. The house is surrounded by six acres of land (used as grazing by the horses) and has several stables and a large yard. In the yard are their vehicles – an Audi saloon, a small pick-up truck, a Peugeot 206 and a Ford Scorpio. The yard is in constant use by a local horse-owner, who rents the stables to break-in new horses and to school them in the purpose-built paddock.

Mr Daniels is a successful businessman, involved in haulage, building materials and plant hire. He owns a large number of excavators and heavy machines, which he leases around the country and his HGVs deliver throughout the UK and sometimes to mainland Europe. He also owns land in and around Ammanford, including a 100-acre site on which he is building a new family home. He is a formidable man, large in stature, and he speaks with a deep booming voice. Mr Daniels is usually wearing soiled working clothes, demonstrating his hands-on approach to his company and, although he is nearing an acceptable age to retire, he invests considerable time in his work and takes great pride in the company he has built. Mrs Daniels is some years younger than her husband and they have been married for over 30 years. She does not have paid employment. She spends much of her time looking after the administrative paperwork that Mr Daniels dislikes so much. Much of the rest of her time is spent around the yard with the horses – she is most often seen wearing her jeans, mucking-out boots and a body warmer. Mrs Daniels enjoys the steady flow of visitors to the house and the yard and the daily routine of taking care of the animals.

They have two sons. John, the older one (29), still lives at home while Steven (24) works for Shell in Aberdeen and offshore, so comes home for a while periodically. Both own high-powered motorcycles and the younger son also has a horse in one of the stables. John is more into the biker culture than Steven is and wears his leathers most of time. He likes to attend bike shows and rallies and had just returned from the Isle of Man TT races. Steven, on the other hand, likes to wear more expensive clothing and likes designer labels. He likes to socialise with his friends when he comes home, and his parents often don't see him for several days.

Mr Daniels and his sons speak Welsh fluently, but Mrs Daniels speaks only English. His family is indigenous to the Amman valley and has had a family business in the area since the 1920s, when they had a farm and then a dairy. Mrs Daniels' father was a publican in the Llandovery area. The household has links with the community through its business ties and their horses. The house and yard are always busy with visitors, employees and other equestrians using the many stables. None of the family has been to university. Mr Daniels attended the local grammar school and worked for the National Coal Board at management level before going it alone. His sons did very well in school, but have followed his lead by going to work from school. The boys have gained vocational qualifications at work and are both at supervisory level in their fields. The family has always run its own businesses and has a strong work ethic based on practical skills and knowledge in engineering and construction.

They watch Welsh-language television and Mr Daniels listens to Classic FM and Radio Cymru, mostly on Sundays. He has been reading *The Western Mail* for over 40 years and still has it delivered every day. He likes to watch Sky News for the business updates when he comes home. The boys buy *Motor Cycle News* and *Backstreet Heroes* from the local newsagent and Mrs Daniels has *Smallholder* magazine delivered. Mr Daniels has begun a subscription to *National Geographic*. The household also has *The Times* delivered daily, and on Sundays they have *The Observer*, *The Sunday Telegraph* and *The Mail on Sunday* delivered. Mr Daniels picks up *The Carmarthen Journal*, *The Ammanford Guardian* and *The South Wales Evening Post* occasionally, but not daily.

The household is a busy one, with activity and visitors throughout the week. The family has a dog and three cats, which roam around the house or sleep in front of the large open fire in the living room. The living room has a patio door that opens up into a large garden which circles the house. The house has a large number of double-glazed windows, including a lovely panoramic window in the living room. There are four bedrooms upstairs and an attic room, in which Mr Daniels keeps a train set.

The house is characterised by an almost cluttered feel. Members of the family have many interests – Mrs Daniels' horses, the sons' motorbikes, and Mr Daniels' steam trains. This is reflected in the large numbers of magazines and newspapers lying around the kitchen, living room, bathrooms and bedrooms. The attic, we were told, is full of back issues of *Motorcycle*, *Autocar* and other magazines. Neither the boys nor Mr Daniels like to throw magazines away. Books, magazines and old newspapers fill the living room, piled under the coffee table, and flowing over the sofa. The living room accommodates a large library of reference books and local history publications, and there are some valuable paintings by a famous local artist (Valerie Ganz) displayed throughout the house. There is a considerable quantity of antique furniture, and the carpets and fittings are all very expensive, but it would not be described as a show home because of its lived-in feel. Nonetheless, there is a underlying feel of quality to the furnishings that suggests that they buy the best quality available.

The kitchen is the first room you enter, and in it is a small television and a radio on the worktop. Mrs Daniels spends much of her time in here, watching different programmes from those Mr Daniels watches in the living room. There are often lovely smells of home-cooked food in the kitchen and one feels drawn to the comfort of this area. In many respects, the kitchen is the focal point of the house and is used as an area to greet and to talk to visitors, or to offer tea or a bacon sandwich. The living room has a high-quality Sharp hi-fi system and a collection of classical records and audio cassettes in the corner. Mr Daniels does not have a CD player but has his collection on vinyl or tape. There is large open fireplace, and beside it a large, wide-screen television, with a VCR beneath in a display cabinet and a Sky digital receiver. The family subscribes to all the sport and film channels at a cost of about £35 per month. There is a television, hi-fi and VCR in each of the boys' bedrooms. They have no PC or Internet access at home. Mrs Daniels has a radio in the stables and there is also a radio in the garage – which is where the older son, John, spends most of his free time with his Harley Davidson motorcycle.

Members of the family have extraordinarily different patterns of media consumption. Mr Daniels mostly watches the news bulletins on Sky and BBC News 24 and reads national broadsheets, while Mrs Daniels watches the HTV news and the ITV evening schedule on terrestrial and reads *The Mail* and the local press. The sons watch films and Eurosport for motorcycle racing. Saturday night is Mr Daniels' night out at the local pub – he usually goes out at around 8 p.m. and returns after midnight. Sunday is Mr Daniels' main day for reading the newspapers and listening to the radio, usually Classic FM. Mrs Daniels is around the stables, and the son(s) are sometimes in the garage tinkering with motorcycles, if they are not riding them. Mrs Daniels likes to have Saturday nights alone in the kitchen with ITV, while the boys tend to be out or in their rooms listening to music.

The household is Welsh-speaking and Welsh is the most spoken language among the men. They all speak English with Mrs Daniels but speak only Welsh to one another. Their Welsh is in a local Amman valley dialect, which is spoken quickly and has become Anglicised to some extent. Mr Daniels regards Welsh as the family's natural tongue, spoken by all of the family's local network. He is of the opinion that speaking Welsh is necessary to be accepted and to get on in the area. He sees the Carmarthen area as *the* Welsh heartland, so the language and its use are very important to him. Although the family identify themselves as Welsh, they do not watch or listen to much Welsh-language broadcasting, although in their locality conversational Welsh is a normal part of their everyday lives.

Davies

Nicola Davies is 27 and has a 5 year old daughter, Louise. She has a casual appearance, wearing jeans and a sports sweater most of the time. She has several gold chains and rings and a striking number of ear piercings. Her daughter seems advanced for her age and her hair and clothes mirror those of her mother. She emulates her mother closely, her eyes following Nicola around the room, and she is never very far from her heels. They live in a rented terraced house near the centre of Cardiff – with three small bedrooms, a living room of two small rooms knocked into one, and a small kitchen. Nicola has always lived in this area of Cardiff, her mother and father live in the street behind and she has many friends living nearby. She feels that it is a close community, but "not somewhere I'd choose to bring up kids". A traditional working class area, in recent years it has experienced some upheaval, as young professionals, students and poor immigrants housed by the local authority have moved in. She says that other local people share her views about the influx of asylum seekers: "There's no money here, why do they want to come here?"

Nicola works part time at a call centre as an administrative assistant. After leaving school she worked in KwikSave, and it is only recently that she has returned to work, with Louise starting school. She works up to 15 hours a week, on Monday, Tuesday and Wednesday. Her former boyfriend, Louise's father, used to work and help her with the rent, but they have recently separated. Their relationship remains somewhat problematic: "He still comes round here now and again to see Louise. I've had trouble with him lately; he keeps coming round at stupid times and that. I can't have that." Starting fieldwork in the household was delayed and difficult because of a series of rows between Nicola and her ex-partner.

Nicola enjoys her work, and her parents pick up Louise from school on the days when Nicola is working. She is still in receipt of housing benefit and family allowance. The job provides her with a little more than she would receive on income support. Nicola has few interests beyond work and home these days, although before Louise was born she used to enjoy socialising and would go out to pubs and nightclubs in Cardiff almost every night. Now she goes out much less than she used to. She says that it is too much hassle and it costs too much. Sometimes she goes to the city centre for a night out with her friends, but not very often. Her mother does not mind babysitting, but she feels that the crowds are getting younger and the clubs have lost their appeal. Occasionally she has friends around and they might bring a video and some beer with them. Perhaps once a week, she and a couple of friends might stay up late watching a film, usually on a Friday. Nicola still has the same group of friends that she had in school and they remain very close, with some of them, like her, having young children.

Occasionally she buys a CD single if she hears something she likes on the radio. She listens mostly to Radio One in the morning on the days that she works. "I like *Sarah Cox*, she's quite good in the morning, she wakes me up and gets me going." She tends to listen to the radio while she and Louise are getting ready for school and work. On Mondays she starts work at 9.30 a.m., so she drops Louise off on her way to work. She works until 5.30 up to three days a week, so her parents pick up Louise, who gets to watch Children's BBC at her grandparents and has some cartoons on video to watch at their house.

Nicola collects Louise from her parents' house after work and usually stays there for some food. During this time, she watches television with her parents and daughter, and reads *The South Wales Echo*, which her mother buys every day. "I usually get home [referring to her mother's house] before *EastEnders*, so I'll watch that and have some tea." She picks up the *South Wales Echo*, but only flicks through the headlines, looks at her stars and sees what is on the television. Nicola does not see herself as someone who really notices what's going on in the media, but she sees herself as a big television viewer, particularly the soaps.

In their own home, Nicola and Louise tend to watch the soaps together. Louise likes *Neighbours*, while Nicola likes *EastEnders*, and they also watch *Coronation Street* and the latest *Soapstars* talent search together. During the week, they tend to go to bed at the same time, around 10.30–11 p.m. She tells us that she only left home to move in with her ex-boyfriend, but now feels that, at 27, she should have independence, although she feels secure that she has friends and family nearby in case she should need them. She likes to feel that her daughter is close to her grandparents, although Louise does not see her father or his parents very often.

The decor is basic, and the living room has a comfortable sofa, which matches a thick-lined pair of blue curtains. The room has a dark-coloured cord carpet and a colourful rug in front of the television. The Social Fund paid for the furniture, with a loan that Nicola took before she started work and is now repaying. The room has pine shelving units, on which are photographs of Louise as a baby and at regular stages since. The latest, a professional school photograph, takes pride of place. The room has an almost utilitarian feel to it – with the furniture in the living room and the table and chairs in the kitchen practical and affordable rather than decorative or expensive. There are very few decorative features around the home in general, and Nicola seems to struggle to fill the space with her belongings. There is a lack of the clutter (old newspapers, clothes, shoes, and so on) that characterises most households.

The living room has a small, silver, Alba television and VCR in the corner, beside which is a small, silver, CD hi-fi unit with speakers. In another corner, behind the sofa, are soft toys, books, dolls and dolls' clothes. Nicola watches television in this room, and Louise plays with her toys when not watching television. The sofa is quite close to the television, and there is a small wooden coffee table on the right side of the sofa on which there are often two or three empty tea mugs. The room has a large window overlooking the terraced street and the busy road can be heard from the room.

In the kitchen Nicola has a radio cassette player, tuned to Radio One, which she listens to over breakfast. There are three kitchen chairs around a small table that is placed against the wall adjoining the living room. There is an open entrance to the living room and sometimes Nicola eats in front of the portable television while Louise is in the other room. Sometimes Nicola watches television in the kitchen while Louise watches a video or plays. Nicola has a full ashtray on the kitchen table and smokes there, away from Louise.

There is also a small portable television in Nicola's bedroom. There are a few Disney videos lying around, including *The Little Mermaid* and *Beauty and the Beast*. There is a small collection of CD singles in the bedroom, mostly chart hits from the last few years – Nicola sometimes buys CDs and VCR tapes from

Woolworths. On the landing by the stairs Nicola keeps an ironing board and there are children's clothes folded into a pile on top of the stairs, and others piled in a plastic wash basket. Although she has her own bedroom, Louise sometimes sleeps with her mother. There is a small single bed for her, along with a small white wardrobe, and there are some plastic animals and soft toys and dolls lying around on the floor. The bedcover and pillowcase have a Barbie motif. The other bedroom is empty, apart from a small chest of drawers.

At 27, Nicola is unusually close to her parents, but she reported that this has not always been the case – over the past five years she has grown closer to her mother in particular. She says that there was a time when she couldn't wait "to get out of that place", but now she finds considerable comfort in the support of her parents. One could see Nicola's rented house as a private space for herself and her daughter, but one close enough to the comfort and support of her extended family. Everyday patterns of activity revolve around the two households, with her own place a space to unwind later in the evening and for having friends around. It represents a practical effort to establish her independence, while her parents provide the safety net she needs since she and her partner split up. The function of the house has changed significantly with the breakdown of her relationship with her ex-partner, so she spends considerably less time there. Owing to her age and the lack of space at her parents' house she continues with her private space, albeit one strongly linked to the extended family home.

Nicola has no doubt that she is Welsh, but she is clear to distinguish herself from Welsh-speakers. When she was younger she regarded those who went to Welsh-medium schools as snobs. She feels bad about this now and would love to learn the language, which she feels she should to be really Welsh, or "proper Welsh". She has no interest in Welsh-language broadcasting, watching S4C for shows such as *Friends* and *Temptation Island*, but never its Welsh-language output. She sees Welsh-language programming as behind the times and not what she would call "streetwise".

None of her peers speaks Welsh and she hated Welsh lessons at school and did not see the point of them. Most of her friends felt the same way, although some of them now wish they could speak it, for their children to learn. Her daughter learns some Welsh at school, but does not speak it at home; she tried, and Nicola felt awkward that she could not help or answer her.

James

Dan y Coed, the James' bungalow, is on the outskirts of Bangor in the village of Talybont, and is reached by a long journey down very windy and narrow country lanes. The household consists of Ieuan and Lucy who are both in their mid fifties, and their sons Gwyn, 29, and Mark, 25, who still live at home. Their oldest son farms near Welshpool. Gwyn uses an extension built onto the house as a small self-contained flat, but he spends most of his time training for bike races and eating in the main part of the house. The house is set off the road and is surrounded by a large yard and drive that slopes down to an entrance which is open, with no gate. There is a minibus, which Ieuan James has from the special school at which he is the headteacher. There is also a silver Citroen ZX that belongs to Mark, the youngest son, and a white Vauxhall Astra which is the family car. Ieuan and Lucy also have a Rover saloon, which is not used much. The house is a large, relatively new, building that was built on the site of an old cottage. It is surrounded on three sides by a large lawn.

Ieuan has a smiling face and a warm manner. He dresses mostly in smart but casual shirts and trousers, not at all old-fashioned, but neither what might be termed the height of fashion. He is a keen amateur dramatics director when he has the time, and enjoys fishing. He is a fluent Welsh speaker. Lucy is a retired opera singer, still very glamorous, with a smart and well-groomed appearance. She has silver-grey hair, is always well-dressed, and works part-time in an office. She is from Birmingham originally and does not speak Welsh. She is happy enough for Ieuan and the boys to speak Welsh to one another, which she does not seem to mind at all, but they converse with her in English,.

Gwyn, 29, is single, a graduate in art and design, and now a semi-pro cyclist who competes throughout the UK and Ireland in road races. He is currently training to represent Wales at the Commonwealth games. He recently performed extremely well in the Welsh national championships. He is of a strong and athletic build, and tends to be dressed in cycling gear, usually having just returned from training.

Mark is 25 and also a keen cyclist. He is studying for a PhD in economic and social development at Liverpool University. Mark is a sports fan and enjoys watching sport as well as participating. He has a steady girlfriend and spends most of his time training, working, or with his girlfriend. He tends to wear sporting or casual gear, such as a rugby shirt and tracksuit bottoms or jeans. Mark participates in a greater range of sports than Gwyn, not just cycling.

The house has a very small kitchen that has a real coffee machine and a small radio on the worktop. You pass through this to a very comfortable and grand living room. At one end is a large mahogany dining table with at least six chairs around it and a plush leather sofa that separates the other half of the room, with two large glass coffee tables in front of the settee and black leather armchairs. Beyond the living room door is a short corridor that leads to the four large bedrooms and the office room. They have to walk through the living room to enter or exit the other, more private, parts of the house. This creates a strong focal feel to the living room, which is amplified by everything being on the ground floor. There is a stronger sense of shared spaces and co-occupation than would be the case with a similarly sized two-story house.

It looks as if considerable energy and finance have been devoted to furnishings and decoration in the living room. The feel is of a household with grown-up children, a home for relaxing in comfort. There are numerous family pictures of the oldest son's children on the wall, and graduation photographs of the boys. There is almost a whole wall and display cabinet full of Gwyn's and Mark's sporting trophies and medals. The living room was the focal point of our visits. The family sat to eat at the table, they drank tea and coffee there, and they often sat in the living room together. Sometimes they leave the room – Ieuan to catch up on some work, and Gwyn to speak to friends on the telephone, sometimes for a long while. The television, hi-fi and satellite systems are all in the far corner of the room, and Lucy was keen to stress that they do not use the television as background but rather as family entertainment when there is something worth watching. Family members spend whatever time they can together in the living room, and often watch videos and talk together in this room.

Ieuan's and Mark's laptops and the PC in Ieuan's study play a part in the fragmentation of the family into separate rooms. The use of these technologies is complemented by family together time when they use the television and VCR as a source of family entertainment – usually a video, or a film on Sky. Both the sons have portable televisions in their rooms and they have a PlayStation between them – which was sometimes in the living room. Surrounding the television set in the living room is a large and eclectic collection of audio CDs, videos, and family games such as Pictionary and Scrabble. There is a radio and a portable television in the kitchen, which they use to listen to or watch the news in the mornings.

They all have very busy lives outside the home. The James family seem very close and relaxed in each other's presence; family unity and time together seems important to them. As a family, they come together for leisure and relaxation by using the television or VCR, viewing as a family. They do not have a television on when they have guests, or when eating together.

Lucy repeatedly commented on their low level of media consumption, and said that the television does not dictate their everyday lives, which seems to be important to her. She feels that television has killed both the art of conversation and creativity. She said that town children get bored much more quickly than country children, and need to be entertained more, instead of entertaining themselves. She felt that the dark image of social life painted by the news media has contributed to people wanting to keep their children at home. All members of the household stress the importance of time together and seemed to feel that the media should be a part of family time. They describe their attitude towards the television as being conditioned by their farming background – they used to own a smallholding in mid Wales when the boys were younger. Ieuan says that the children were always doing something outside, or they had animals to feed, so they have always had a busy life. On a Saturday morning there would be no television and they would go fishing or "get out there and do something". Their lifestyle now seems to follow from their life as farmers. As Mark said, "it's ingrained in us". This family history helps to make sense of the home set-up, with the lads still living at home and the closeness of the unit perhaps shaped by their collective and interdependent roles on the farm.

Newspapers and radio play an important part in everyday life. Ieuan likes to listen to Radio Cymru in the car on the way to work and used to pick up a copy of *The Daily Post* during the day – now that Lucy works less she usually goes out and buys it. Mark tends to watch Sky News a lot in the morning, and Gwyn tends to watch the Discovery Channel for an hour in the mornings. The news punctuates their day and with BBC News 24 they were able to follow the election because of its brief and regular synopses. The family, in particular Mark, likes the flexibility and availability of 24-hour news reports. Mark reads *The Western Mail* occasionally, when there is a big sporting event, but mostly he buys *The Guardian*, especially if he is taking the train to Liverpool University. Lucy tends to read *The Daily Post* when Ieuan returns home, mainly for the local news and television listings. She watches *Bad Girls* on ITV and listens to Classic FM every day around lunchtime.

The male (and Welsh) members of the household expressed strong views about the media in Wales. Ieuan sees the Welsh national news as focused on south Wales, with very little of local interest, very few local news stories. They get local news and information from one of the large number of local newspapers which they have read in the recent past – the *Caernarfon and Denbigh Herald*, the *Bangor and Anglesey Mail*, the *North Wales Chronicle*, *The Pioneer* and *Llais Ogwan*. Mark tends to watch the international news on Sky to "find out what's going on" and feels that the Welsh news is not relevant, except for sport. He said that the

Welsh national news is neither local enough nor global enough to make him sit and watch. Ieuan and Mark saw the political and media culture of Wales as southern-centric, and feel neglected by the media because of geography and demography.

The family was concerned that the negative way in which the Assembly is reported contributed to the low turn-out for the referendum. Ieuan said that he felt that most people have a negative image of the work of the Assembly because we "don't really know what's going on behind the scenes … that's why people feel dissatisfied with it". While the Assembly constitutes something newsworthy, the general attitude is negative, and for Ieuan the media are in part responsible for this.

Regarding the BBC, Ieuan said that there was a prevailing centralism, a London bias – in political terms and in regional BBC policy – so reporting was not objective. He thought that the BBC gives the perspective from London. He thought, and Mark agreed, that S4C has a more rounded and multi-perspective approach to Assembly news, using far more academic opinions as well as conducting more journalistic enquiry.

Lewis

Karen Lewis is in her early forties, a fluent Welsh speaker living in Builth Wells. She has short dark hair and brown eyes and dresses smartly for work, but always casually in the house. She works full-time as a secretary and has three children, Dafydd (18) and Rhodri (15) (from her first marriage) and Hannah (8) (from her second). Karen is from Ystalefera in the Swansea Valley, but has lived in the area for nearly 18 years. He first husband was a farmer and they lived on a farm of nearly 500 acres. She has been at her job for the last five years and before that was a full-time housewife. Karen has 'A' levels in Welsh, Drama and Music. Before getting married, she wanted to go to college to become a teacher. She still wants to take a degree, but feels that she cannot afford it until the children are grown up.

She has recently separated from her second husband and lives with the children in a three-story townhouse that has seven bedrooms and three bathrooms. Her sons are still at school, the oldest studying for 'A' levels, and her daughter is at the local primary school. Karen has little time for her own hobbies, but enjoys taking her daughter swimming or to the park, especially at weekends. Karen gets frequent visits from her parents, who travel up from Ystalefera.

Dafydd, the oldest son, enjoys sports and likes to play snooker with his friends.

He usually dresses in a shirt or tee-shirt and a pair of jeans. Like most boys of his age, he likes to buy nice clothes to go out in, and always has to have the latest trainers. He is learning to drive and cannot wait to have his freedom. When he is not in school or out with his friends, Dafydd spends most of his time in his room or in the living room in front of the television.

Rhodri is much quieter than his older brother. He, too, likes rugby and plays for the local youth team. He also goes out at weekends to Builth Wells, but is less fashion-conscious than his brother and prefers to wear a Welsh rugby shirt most of the time. Rhodri likes his PlayStation and also likes to be in front of the television or computer screen.

Hannah wears her school uniform most of the time, though at the weekend she might wear a dress, but more often a jogging-type suit with a hood top. She loves to go swimming at the local pool, and watches Children's BBC with her mother when she gets home from school.

The family are a mix of rural and urban in many respects. All of them except Hannah have lived on farms at some point, either with parents and/or through marriage, but they now live in the centre of a rural town. The house is in the centre of Builth Wells, near the high school, detached and three storeys tall like the others in the street. Karen has no mortgage but has to support the family on her single wage. The house has a large grass garden with a small shed that is filled with the Hannah's toys and gets a lot of use. There is a small plastic slide in the back garden, and an array of plastic spades and buckets is strewn around the paved area next to the back door. The kitchen is modern and is also used as a play area; it is where Karen and Hannah spend much of their time together. There is a large doll's house near the kitchen table. The house is spacious and fresh, yet lived in. Two teenage sons are evident, with sports kit and training shoes littering the house. Given the toys around the house, it is a remarkable feat to keep order at all. One gets the feeling that it is a happy and busy house.

All the children have a television in their bedrooms, and the boys have a VCR and hi-fi too. There are two televisions downstairs, one of which – in the front room – is used solely to watch videos and for the PlayStation. This room is primarily for the boys. The boys' living room is full of videos, mostly comedy and sport, with the occasional Disney film for Hannah. Other titles included the *Aliens Trilogy*, the BBC Wales comedy *Grand Slam* and the American series *Friends*. There are also several rugby and soccer videos on the shelves, along with dozens of paperback and hardback books belonging to the whole family. This is where most of the television viewing takes place. It is a small room and is the central hub of the house in many respects, even though it is one of the smallest spaces.

There is another living room, which Karen tends to occupy more than the other members of the family. This is painted white with two small floral patterned sofas that each accommodate two people. There is a doll's house with furniture in one corner and a small television and VCR in the other corner above a cupboard. The room faces the street and has net curtains and thick velvet curtains that are tied back. The room has a feminine feel, with china ornaments, figures and tea and dinner sets that look valuable and are displayed on a grand dresser near the door. There are photographs of the children and other family members on display. The room is used by Karen as a place for her to read and relax. It is used as the more formal of the two living rooms – the one for visitors.

There is a small radio in the kitchen that is heavily used in the mornings and early evenings. The kitchen area is bright and gets a considerable amount of sun during the day. It is a good place for Karen to keep an eye on what Hannah is doing in the garden.

There is a PC with Internet capability in a study on the second floor, which Karen uses for work and the boys use for homework and getting information from the Internet. Karen says that she prefers encyclopaedias and reference books to the Internet. The boys surf the net and occasionally buy goods online.

The family used to have Sky, but they stopped their subscription because it cost too much – which was partly because they had two dishes, one for upstairs and the other for downstairs. Karen is considering re-subscribing to Sky in the near future, or buying a DVD player. She is reluctant to pay for any more services, but the boys are really keen to have Sky again. She does not know how much longer she can last before she bows to the pressure. Since they have been without Sky, Karen has noticed that they spend much more on going out to the cinema and at the local video hire store. She feels it would be as cheap to subscribe again.

Karen describes herself as a "channel-hopper", and says that she prefers to read and does not watch a lot of television because there is very little that deserves her time and attention. She watches *Pobol y Cwm* on S4C and *EastEnders* on BBC1 on a regular basis. The family sometimes watches *EastEnders*, other soaps or the news together. She reads the *Independent on Sunday*, and *The Western Mail* at work. She prefers these newspapers to the tabloids as she feels that they go into the news stories in some depth and avoid sensationalism and gossip – something she associates with *The Sun* and *The Mirror* and which she dislikes. She began to read *The Western Mail* because they take it at work, but she now reads it on a regular basis and takes it home. She listens to Radio Cymru and Radio Four. She says that her radio and newspaper choices are influenced a great deal by her job, where she speaks Welsh and is in contact with the rural Welsh-speaking community on a daily basis. She feels that Radio Cymru, especially *Stondin Sulwyn*, is particularly good.

The boys like anything to do with sport, particularly rugby. They associate good Welsh sports coverage with S4C and tend to watch this channel for programmes such as *Sgorio* and international match coverage. The boys also like a host of car and motorcycle events and follow these on Sky Eurosport. They enjoy spending time on their father's farm and are unlike some teenagers in that they are relatively hard working, especially at weekends. Where they live they are able to venture into public houses and consume alcohol at a young age. There is a strong culture of alcohol among youngsters in the area, which the boys have embraced. Karen herself recognises that this is normal for boys around here and that they could be "up to worse things, like drugs".

The oldest son cannot wait to finish his 'A' levels so that he can move to Cardiff to study. Many of the boys in Builth Wells have gone there. He seems keen to experience more than the rural heartlands of Wales have to offer. It is symptomatic of places like Builth Wells that the population is an ageing one, and that the boys already have one eye on getting out.

They live in an area of Powys that is heavily Anglicised, so their sense of Welsh identity is connected with keeping the language alive. Their sense of Welsh national identity is strong because of the language and their roots in south Wales. Karen and the two boys are fluent Welsh speakers, while the daughter has a limited Welsh-language capability. Her second husband was English, so the use of Welsh in the house was restricted and infrequent. Her Welsh is near-perfect: she and the boys speak Welsh a lot more these days, although the younger son is hardly fluent because of lack of practice, while the daughter is picking it up well. Karen actively encourages the children to speak Welsh and they all are beginning to speak to her in Welsh, but not among themselves. The family's use of Welsh seems to have suffered as a result of the linguistic mix of the family over recent years, and this is reflected in their varying levels of ability. They feel somewhat dislocated from the Welsh-speaking heartland from where they originate.

Powell

The Powells live in the Llandaf area of Cardiff. Rhian Powell is a human resources manager for a city bank and her husband Brian is a self-employed optometrist. They have two children, Gareth (16) and Anne (19). Anne left for university during the course of our research. The family all speak Welsh fluently. Rhian Powell is a diminutive figure with a large presence. She has a friendly and warm personality and a smart corporate appearance. She enjoys gardening and cooking when she has the time. She feels outnumbered by males now that her daughter has gone away to university. Rhian has a degree in business studies and has been involved with ongoing study in connection with her work – she also has a Masters in Human Resources. Brian is in his early fifties and talks of early retirement in a few years. He is of slim build with silver hair, likes to keep fit by playing squash and golf, and loves his car and motoring in general. Last year he and Rhian went to Thailand for a fortnight's holiday. Gareth is still at school doing 'A' levels (Economics, IT, French and Mathematics), and has a keen interest in sport. He plays rugby for the local side and the school team, on the wing, and is learning to drive.

The Powells' house is large, white and detached, set back from one of the main roads heading west out of Cardiff towards the Vale of Glamorgan. The front garden is surrounded by conifer trees, which obscure outside views of their trim lawn and pond with water features. The front of the house has a large driveway, but no garage. The family has two cars: Brian drives a BMW 3 series saloon, while Rhian has a company car, a Rover 200. They have a large back garden, into which they have extended the house with a conservatory, which provides an additional living room. The house has four bedrooms, plus an attic that they have converted into a guest room. There is a generous living room, which backs onto the conservatory and garden, and the kitchen is a farmhouse design with a Rayburn-style gas cooker. The kitchen and living room give a rural feel to the house, despite its urban location. The house is furnished in neutral colours with large floral-style sofas, which give the living areas a clean and comfortable feel. In contrast, the children's bedrooms are cluttered and individualised with an array of gadgets, books, magazines and posters, which distinguish their space from the rest of the house.

Gareth is normally home first, unless he has rugby practice when he comes home at around 7 p.m. Rhian normally gets in at about 6.30 p.m., about half an hour after Brian. Gareth usually makes himself something to eat and sits in the living room eating and watching the television until his parents arrive home. The news usually fills the space in the living room at this time – usually BBC News 24 via Sky. Rhian usually has *The Daily Mail* in the kitchen and she flicks through this before embarking on the evening meal for her and Brian. On Wednesdays, Brian plays squash and Rhian visits friends or her mother, who lives about 20 minutes away. Gareth catches up with homework, procrastinating with the odd video in his bedroom and a few games on the PlayStation – he likes racing games like *Colin McRae Rally*.

Brian and Rhian like to sit together in the living room watching the news while they each talk about their day at work. On most evenings members of the family eat together – when Gareth has rugby his parents wait for him before eating. During the summer months, they eat in the conservatory, but they also have a large dining room that has space for a dinner party and more. At the weekend Gareth normally plays rugby and Brian plays golf and, especially on Sundays, the family has a late dinner together. They all have quite busy lives, so each of them has time to use the media devices in the house at times when they know that the others will be out or engaged in some other activity.

There are several areas where the media are used. The kitchen has a small radio-cassette player, which is normally tuned to Radio Two or Radio Wales. The kitchen is not the focal point of the house, but is used as an area to prepare food quickly. The radio is used here as a background to cooking. Rhian sometimes reads the newspaper with the radio on in the kitchen, but does not spend a lot of time relaxing in the kitchen.

They tend to use the living room and conservatory for sitting and reading the newspaper or watching television. The living room houses the wide-screen television, VCR, DVD player and the Sky digital receiver. There is a large collection of videos, including musicals, comedy, action and sports. Brian uses the VCR to record programmes like *Top Gear*, but mainly likes to watch the news. He keeps his daily newspapers by the side of the chair. He reads *The Western Mail* on most days, mainly for the Welsh news and business reports, and he really likes the 'Motoring' section on a Friday. Rhian sometimes watches *EastEnders* or reads a book – she does not watch that much television, but enjoys UK Gold and UK Living on Sky. Like Brian, Rhian likes to sit and watch television at the end of the evening, for an hour or so before bed. This is her time to relax; often she spends an hour earlier in the evening in the dining room working on the PC. Brian also uses the PC occasionally, to keep accounts and sometimes to surf the Web for information on cars or to use online auctions. The dining room sometimes doubles as an office during the week. It is the room where household members use the PC, and sometimes the Internet, and get some space from the others to do so. The conservatory is used as a dining area, so the dining room is rarely used unless they have guests around.

Gareth spends most of the time in his room during the evening, although he too uses the PC – for his homework or to surf the Web. Gareth has a television and VCR in his room, as well as a hi-fi. He has a collection of CDs, most of which lie on the floor, with stacks of car magazines. He has a Six Nations rugby poster on his door and one of the Stereophonics from a live concert he went to at Cardiff Castle. He also has a PlayStation in his room, with *G-Police*, *Tekken 3*, *Final Fantasy 7*. He likes to spend time in the room, because he wants to be away from his parents and thinks their taste in television is poor. He watches *Top Gear* on BBC1 and *Driven* on S4C with his father in the living room, but most of his contact with the rest of the household during the evening is to eat or to come downstairs to take telephone calls from his friends, particularly his girlfriend.

The family occasionally watches a film together in the living room, and Gareth uses the DVD player to watch films hired from Blockbuster. Each member of the household uses the living room for their own specialist activity (for example, listening to music or watching a film), usually when one or more of the others are out of the house. Their busy routines and social lives outside the household make conflict over space rare. They tend to work around each other and make use of the time and space effectively for their own ends. This has become easier since Anne has gone to university.

The Powells can all speak Welsh but they converse with one another almost exclusively in English. They use the occasional word of Welsh to one another but do not use the language at home in any extended way. Gareth goes to a Welsh-medium school, and his and Anne's Welsh is significantly more fluent than that of their parents. Rhian and Brian had conversational Welsh passed down from their parents, to whom they speak Welsh, and they can understand Welsh-language programmes on S4C. Rhian watches *Pobol y Cwm* in the week and Brian watches the rugby in Welsh on S4C.

They tend to listen to Radio Wales in the kitchen and in the conservatory while they read the newspapers during weekday evenings and weekend mornings. They like to listen to *Roy Noble* and *Wales at One*, sometimes switching to Radio Two if they feel like music rather than chat or news.

They have *The Western Mail* delivered daily, and sometimes buy *Wales on Sunday*. This competes with *The Observer* and *The Mail on Sunday* in the household, although the newspapers are bought for different reasons. Brian likes *The Western Mail* because it represents the area in which they live. Its focus is on national issues, economic and political, and he feels that the newspaper represents his social and economic group in Wales. He likes the fact that it is a national newspaper for Wales and that its focus on the south (and the south-east in particular). He does not buy any local newspapers, but sees *The Western Mail* as a Welsh counterpart to the London dailies, with enough local and national content to give it a distinctive Welsh stamp.

Gareth reads the 'Sport' sections of *The Western Mail*, and loves *Y Clwb Rygbi* on S4C; he followed the Lions tour on the Welsh channel. He watches *Sgorio* and used to watch *Pam fi, Duw?*, but has not recently. He sees Welsh-language television as a vital part of Welsh culture, but admits that he feels reluctant to watch it because of the number of sport and music channels available on Sky. He feels that Welsh-language programmes cannot compete for his attention because they cater for the older generation most of the time.

The family has an unusual sense of Welshness. They are very keen to stress their Welsh-language background, but want to show even more that they are a *modern* Welsh family, adapting to the changing nature of south-east Wales. Brian stresses the importance of sending their children to a Welsh-medium school but, equally, emphasises modern languages, economics and IT skills. Their ability to speak Welsh sets them apart from most families on their street, but they are keen to stress their progressive and professional ideals. They stress that their ability to speak Welsh gives them a certain status, and certainly gives Anne and Gareth some advantages. In many respects they represent a new culture in Wales, in which the language is not necessarily associated with traditional communities and occupations, but rather with a mobile and educated professional class.

Protheroe

Geoff and Angharad Protheroe live in Colwinston in the Vale of Glamorgan, just off the A48. Geoff is a 63 year old retired bank manager and his wife Angharad is retired from her business, but works part-time as a dinner lady at the local primary school. They live in a beautiful detached house with a back garden that overlooks the rolling fields towards Rhoose and Barry. Their house is set off the road in this quiet village. They have a Peugeot 406 estate in the driveway. The house has a grand conservatory at the back, which is used as a multi-purpose room. It is a dining area, and a family area when their grandchildren come around. The house is beautifully decorated with original artworks from west Wales and there is a very interesting antique gramophone in the hallway. The house has three bedrooms, a large kitchen and bathrooms upstairs and down-stairs.

They have a son and daughter, both married, and three grandchildren. They own another property in the south of France and like to take the children out there during the school holidays. Having retired, Geoff has a keen interest in stocks and shares, and in antique auctions – to pick up bargains for future sale. Angharad likes her work at the school, because it is local and she likes to be around the children. She says it makes her feel young. Angharad likes cooking and Geoff likes to bring wine back from France. They tend to have elaborate meals and always made us feel welcome with offers of tempting dishes.

Geoff helps his daughter by taking the children to school each day, so he gets up at around 7.30 a.m. Normally he has breakfast in the kitchen and reads *The Western Mail*, which they have delivered. He goes straight to the public notices and financial news to look at future developments and business opportunities. He tells me that this is a habit from his banking days, when he would look to see who was insolvent, or for new investment opportunities. He leaves the newspaper on the kitchen table for Angharad to read. They always have *The Western Mail* delivered and have done so since they can remember. Their own parents used to read the newspaper and they both identify with it and are highly loyal to it. They also have *The Daily Telegraph* delivered, which they both tend to read in the evening. Geoff usually reads it first, while Angharad reads *The Western Mail* in the kitchen. Whoever reads it first puts it in the newspaper holder by the side of the armchair in front of the television.

Their days are quite full because Geoff also picks the grandchildren up from school and brings them back to the house until their daughter and son-in-law call to collect them after work. Thus the extended family meets most evenings during the week, and quite often eats together – so the house is quite vibrant, with grandchildren enthusiastically telling their grandparents what they have learnt at school. The Protheroes are close to their family and obviously like to spend time with each other; they regularly go to France together. When the grandchildren come in from school they like to talk to their grandparents. The television is not used as a babysitter, though the children do like to switch it on. They like Fox Kids because of the cartoons. This gives Angharad some time to prepare food. Geoff normally tends his vegetable patch in the nice weather or sits and reads with the children.

Later in the evenings, on their own again, they will settle down together to watch some television. They like to watch the news on BBC News 24 or Sky. They still watch mainly terrestrial television and do not really know how the interactive and digital channels work. They only bought the system so that they could transfer the card to their receiver in France, thus picking up all the British channels. The Protheroes do not consider themselves heavy television viewers although, when they do switch on, they are surprised at how much they engage with programmes, especially Angharad with the soaps.

Angharad likes *Pobol y Cwm* and *EastEnders*. She says that *Pobol y Cwm* reminds her of her home village in west Wales. Geoff, on the other hand, likes to watch the Discovery channel and Men and Motors – he used to co-pilot a rally car, many years ago. Both enjoy cookery programmes such as *Food and Drink* on BBC2 and *Rhodes Around Britain*.

They have a large living room with a CD hi-fi system, a television, a VCR and a Sky digital receiver. The living room is the main place for watching television. They have access to over 60 channels, including films and sport. Although they watch rarely, they like to have a choice, so that there is always something of interest when they want it. Geoff occasionally likes to sit in the corner chair and listen to music. He has a collection of CDs and vinyl 12-inch records which he keeps in a small cabinet. Most of the CDs are collections of hits from the 50s and 60s, along with some classical recordings. They use this room as an area to unwind in, as most of their entertaining takes place in the large conservatory. The living room is long and is divided into two by a large sofa. In front of the sofa is the television and front window, with another sofa and armchair to the left. However, behind is another smaller sofa with a coffee table in front of it. It is as if the room is divided into personal or intimate spaces, with additional seating for when they have guests.

The conservatory is fitted with a large round dining table, expensive lighting and comfortable chairs. It is light and has great views, and it is where guests are entertained and meals eaten. When they have guests they sometimes retire to the living room but, more often, only use the living room when alone, to watch television. They spend most evenings in the conservatory, taking their time enjoying their food and wine. The conservatory is a family room, a space in which to enjoy their retirement, and a symbol of the wealth they have accrued.

The kitchen is a busy area, which Angharad makes her own. She was brought up in a farming family and likes to cook large elaborate meals, enough to feed a full house. She loves the kitchen and has spent years kitting it out, having a new kitchen fitted every few years. She loves to cook and, most of all, to have a nice kitchen. She enjoys having friends and family around and preparing a large feast for them. Angharad and Geoff use the kitchen to have a quick cup of coffee or tea and to read the newspaper during their busy early morning hours. Angharad has *The Western Mail* in the kitchen, laid out on the table, so that she can scan its broad pages as she prepares food. One advantage of the newspaper is that it fills the table, so she can scan it at a glance.

They have a PC in their bedroom, but it is used rarely. They bought it on their son's recommendation, and occasionally have shopped online at tesco.com. They have also used it to keep in touch with relatives and friends in France, at a lower cost than the telephone. They have researched holiday destinations online, but have not booked online yet. They like online shopping and auctions, firstly because there are no salesmen and, secondly, because you can take your time before ordering, while also having full specifications and facts on screen. The PC's location, in the bedroom, reflects its low use. In fact, it is no longer even connected, and the monitor is in the closet.

The Protheroes feel a close affinity to *The Western Mail*. The newspaper has been in their families since they can remember, and both agree that they would feel lost without it. It represents their views on Welsh issues and has always reflected their view of themselves as Welsh. As they see it, the newspaper has changed in recent years, but so have they. The newspaper has modernised, becoming a less rural newspaper, but reflecting the changing nature of Wales and the Welsh. They feel the same affinity to the newspaper now as they have always done. When they lived in London they used to have *The Western Mail* sent to them every day. The newspaper represented a way of maintaining a sense of Welsh identity in England, and a link with Welsh events.

Angharad watches a little Welsh-language television and listens to Radio Wales, though Geoff is less interested in Welsh-language broadcasting. She listens to *Good Evening Wales* on Radio Wales, while Geoff is more involved with *The Western Mail* and *The Daily Telegraph*. He likes to watch the news rather than listen to it on the radio. He wants a mix of national and global news, whereas Angharad is more focused on local and national news – on radio and in the press. Angharad's identity is constructed in far more local terms than is that of Geoff. For Geoff, his core identification is his standing as a retired bank manager.

Both speak Welsh, although neither their children nor grandchildren do, and they seem to speak it only because they were brought up with the language. Angharad speaks it to her family back in west Wales, for example on the telephone. They did not speak to each other in Welsh when we were present, though they reported that they occasionally speak it to one another around the house. Geoff is very clear that he is a fluent Welsh speaker, despite apparently not using the language. They said that their Welsh is not 'media Welsh' but the language that was spoken by people when they grew up. They saw Welsh-language programming, particularly for children, as a good thing, and connected it with the growth in the number of people speaking Welsh. Geoff demonstrates that claims to speak the language encompass a great diversity of linguistic ability. The Protheroes are Welsh speakers who for reasons of lack of ability or practice feel more comfortable speaking to one another exclusively in English. Nonetheless they see the language as the main identifier of the Welsh people – it makes them feel different and (for example) stand out when they are abroad. They both acknowledge the Welsh language as a part of their life stories, but feel that their time in London and abroad has given them a broader perspective; the Welsh language relates more to their past.

Riley

The Rileys have lived on the southern outskirts of Wrexham, in Flintshire, for over 25 years. Their bungalow straddles the rural–urban border and has a village feel, but with access to the town centre and the main routes to the north-west of England. Richard Riley is 60, a retired teacher, and his wife Julie Riley is 57 and still teaches, though is near to retirement. Richard is short but well-built, balding on top, with some grey hair around the sides. He likes to wear his favourite light-coloured trousers and comfortable trainers around the place. He often wears a light-coloured, half-sleeved shirt. Julie is slim, with reading glasses permanently around her neck, and silvery blonde hair. She often dresses more formally than Richard, wearing a casual suit to work and often not having time to change until much later. Richard was born in south-west England and his parents moved to Wales when he was very young – his mother was Welsh and wanted to move back to north Wales when he was born. He says that he regards himself as Welsh because he was brought up in Wales. Julie was born and brought up in Wales, in a small village near the border with Shropshire. They met one another at Liverpool University.

Richard is a keen gardener and the most noticeable feature of the large bungalow is its large well-kept garden, with a dazzling array of colours and year-round flowers. They have recently bought a new blue Ford Focus, which Richard cleans on Sunday morning. They have a Dalmatian, Stella, and it is usually after she has been in the car that the back seats need a good clean.

The garden is immaculate, with a small varnished wooden shed in the corner near to the back door. There is a patio area near the kitchen door at the back and they like to have friends around for a barbeque in the summer. Their daughters have left home: one now lives with her husband in Canada and the other is working in Cardiff. Richard has plenty of time on his hands to do the garden and to take the dog for a walk. Richard travels to see musical perform-ances at a local arts centre when he gets the chance – he really enjoys watching and listening to jazz in nice surroundings, although he does not play a musical instrument himself. Julie enjoys yoga once a week with a work colleague, and teaches piano several times a week. Both are involved with the local Catholic church, which they attend twice each Sunday.

The Rileys enjoy travel and try to get away as much as they can. They have been to South America, where they walked the Inca trail in Peru, and to Thailand, Canada and Africa in the last few years. They feel lucky that teaching has given them the chance to travel and to broaden their horizons. They have an extensive collection of photographs from their holidays and numerous artefacts and trinkets that they have picked up along the way. "We're not really beach holiday people; we like to get out and see the place and do something with our time", they said.

The house is open plan, has three bedrooms and feels very spacious for a bungalow. The kitchen area doubles as the dining room and has a tiled floor, giving it a clean but cool feel. From the kitchen a corridor leads down the hall, with a bathroom on the right, a bedroom straight ahead, and another bedroom to the right. The corridor is painted magnolia and there are dried flowers and herbs hanging from the wall, and family photographs and paintings along the way. Second on the right is the living room, at the front of the house. The living room is quite small, but comfortable and thickly carpeted. It has a piano in one corner, two settees, a coffee table, a modest television and a VCR in the other corner. The room's ambience is set by classical music: Julie teaches piano and loves music, while Richard enjoys listening to the classics and some contemporary jazz. There is a hi-fi system with headphones plugged in by the side of one of the big armchairs, and next to it a collection of classical CDs (Bach, Mozart, Grieg) and also some classic jazz (Gillespie, Miles Davies). The system looks well-used, more so perhaps than the television, which is housed in a glass cabinet. The walls are covered with family portraits and photographs and there is a dresser that holds a collection of graded music sheets and theory books. There are numerous small souvenirs picked up from market places on their holidays, including small figurines from Peru that depict various indigenous deities in weird and wonderful positions. There is a small South American mask above the fireplace that depicts a deity, which they say is derived from a hybrid of Inca and Catholic religions.

Richard and Julie Riley spend quite a lot of their time at home during the week and spend much of it together. Three nights a week Julie has children to the house for hour-long piano lessons and during this time Richard will take the dog for a walk, or sometimes go to the local for a pint and a chat. Julie finds her weekly yoga class relaxing, but does not push herself too hard – it is more of a social thing. Richard spend his days around the house doing small jobs and tending the garden. He says he would take up golf, but hates that type of person.

He prefers to be with the dog on a long walk. His shed houses some half-finished wooden cabinets and turned wood, which he works on and gives to friends and neighbours. He has become quite involved with activities at their church since he retired and spends some of his time organising events for the younger and elderly members of the church. He and his wife are also involved with organising social gatherings and days out as a part of the social life of the church.

During the evening they tend to share the cooking, with Radio Four or Classic FM on in the background. They have *The Daily Post* delivered each weekday and *The Observer* on Sunday. They both like the local newspaper for forthcoming events and to keep up with local news. Sunday morning is the time when they sit together in the kitchen and read the newspaper over breakfast. They do not read the 'Sport' or 'Business' sections very much, but are interested in travel and the arts. They buy it mainly for its coverage of international events. They both have a keen interest in world economic and social development and have considered opinions on global events and news. The Rileys read *The Times Education Supplement* as a matter of habit, for its debate of the future of teaching and education.

The kitchen is where the Rileys like to sit and chat, sometimes reading the newspaper or listening to the radio. The radio usually accompanies any cooking that goes on – both of them like to cook and both like Classic FM because it has more music and less chat. Sometimes when reading the newspaper, Richard has discussion programmes on Radio Four on in the background. He says that it is like being in the staff room at school, where you can listen to other people's voices but keep your own counsel at the same time. Richard also has a radio in the shed and this, too, is tuned to Classic FM.

The living room is used for piano lessons in the evening, at which times Richard goes out with the dog. Later in the evening the Rileys will sit together in the living room and watch some television – they have only terrestrial and do not watch it much. They receive no Welsh broadcasting, but *Granada* and Channel 4. They watch the ITV *News at Ten* as a matter of course. They enjoy the late evening together (with the dog), and usually go to bed quite early, after the news unless there is a film or a documentary of special interest on television. They like to watch *Horizon* on BBC2 and sometimes *Newsnight* (more so since the eleventh of September). The Rileys enjoy cookery programmes and watch *Gary Rhodes Around Britain* and, occasionally, *The Naked Chef*, both on BBC2.

Occasionally Julie watches *EastEnders*, during which Richard will put on his headphones and shut it out with some music. Alternatively, if Richard wants to watch something, Julie might go into the bedroom and use the PC to email their daughter in Canada. They have AOL unmetered Internet access for £14.99 a month. They only subscribed in order to have regular contact with their daughter and it was she who suggested a computer as a cheaper means of communication. One or both of them email their daughter, or send some pictures to her, at least once a week. The daughter and her family have been in Canada for just over a year and they keep in regular contact – the Rileys have just returned from a trip to Toronto. The Internet was the main reason they gave for buying a computer, and getting to grips with the technology is something that Richard enjoys.

The Rileys regard themselves as Welsh. Although they do not speak the language, or receive Welsh-language broadcasting, they position themselves in opposition to those across the nearby border. The closeness to the border means that their sense of Welsh identity is quite strong in that they distinguish themselves from the people of Chester and Liverpool. They stressed the differences in their accent from that of Chester and Liverpool, which they see as the stereotype of northerners by those in the south of England. The Rileys dislike the fact that people in South Wales regard them as sounding like 'scousers'. They see themselves as more open to those across the border than are people in north-west Wales. They do not see themselves as nationalists nor do they regard speaking Welsh as the defining characteristic of Welshness. So, their sense of Welshness is defined in terms of opposition to England, and is perhaps a softer form of Welshness compared with our households in Gwynedd or Carmarthen. However, the close proximity of the border has a sharpening effect on their sense of national identity.

Thus although the Rileys identify themselves as Welsh, they do not see themselves as tied to any stereotype but, rather, see themselves as open-minded and liberal people. Many of their neighbours are English and they said that their village was a cultural mix, a hybrid of Welsh and English. They display a sense of identity that is closely linked to England but rooted firmly in Wales.

Swaine

The Swaines live in the centre of Merthyr Tydfil. The house is deceptively large; it looks very small from the outside but has four bedrooms. The terrace is very narrow, making parking very difficult. They do not own a car, but sometimes borrow one from Michelle's father to take the children somewhere. Michelle and John are married and have a son and daughter. They live within a mile and a half of their work and the children's school, and walk to work each day.

John is a shift worker at a furniture factory making office furniture for the armed forces and bulk orders for overseas. He is 30 but looks slightly older because he has a receding hairline. He is of small stature, with dark hair, and is quietly spoken. He dresses in an old tracksuit around the house, and jeans and a shirt for work. He was born and raised in the Merthyr area.

Michelle is 29 and works as a sales assistant at Boots the chemist in the centre of Merthyr. She works full-time and cares for the children after school. Michelle is usually dressed in her work uniform. She too was born and raised in Merthyr, and her parents and sister live within walking distance.

Amy (aged 8) could not be described as shy! She likes to show off and John and Michelle both agree that she will end up on the stage! She is a lively girl who likes to sing and talk. She spends some time each night with other children from the terrace playing in the street. Amy is a tall girl for her age and wears brightly coloured plastic jewellery and hair clips.

Christopher is 7 and a busy child; he takes up a considerable amount of his parents' time because of his behaviour. He tends to kick a football around indoors and is constantly talked to, to modify his actions. On most of our visits he was running around, still dressed in his school uniform.

Most of their time at the weekend is spent at home or visiting Michelle's parents for Sunday lunch. The weekends were regarded as the main family time. Neither John nor Michelle get out much in a social capacity

The household is a very busy one, with children from the street popping in and out to investigate our researcher's presence and car! During our time there, on every visit, the television remained on; this was the only household where this was the case. The terrace is very close-knit, according to Michelle, and it has an atmosphere of familiarity, with many doors open and individuals engaged in conversation on the door-step. John's view is the complete opposite. He feels that there is no sense of community in the street. This may show the effect of John's shift patterns on his social contact.

They have a modestly sized living room that was formerly two small rooms that have been knocked into one. By the front window the children have a pool table set up, and in the lounge section is a large television with Sky and a VCR, which takes up a considerable amount of room. This is the main focus of the room and the television is always on. The television, and specifically Sky, is the staple of the household. There is a home computer in the front area of the living room that they say they use occasionally, but it has no Internet capability and seems rather redundant. There are televisions in each of the bedrooms, and Amy has a VCR in her bedroom too. There is a small radio in the kitchen and a hi-fi in the living room. The children have separate rooms, where they have shared use of a Gameboy and Sony PlayStation.

The house is in the process of being decorated and John is busy painting the kitchen. The living room and upstairs are clean and nicely decorated, but there is no common design aesthetic, although they seem to be buying the best they can afford. The house is cluttered with children's toys, footballs, guns and Disney videos. The main use of the media in the household is to entertain the children, rather than a news or information service. They do not watch a lot of news. John has *The Sun* delivered daily, and later he swaps this with his father-in-law for *The Welsh Mirror*. Michelle tends to pick up and skim through whatever newspaper is lying around. Neither Michelle nor John have much interest in the Welsh news or local newspapers, and they have a negative or uninterested view of Wales and the language, local news and local events. Sky or the VCR is used as a constant background to family routines such as eating, bathing and playing. Use of the media is not very selective, but a means to an end.

John watches a lot of sport on his own, because of his shift work, during the week. At the weekend he likes to watch football on Sky, and to do small jobs around the house. Occasionally they watch films on Sky Box Office or Sky Movies, if John and Michelle are alone, or when the grandparents have the children for the evening. The household mainly watches the film, cartoon and sports channels on Sky (Sky Sports, Sky Box Office, Sky Movies, The Children's Channel, Fox Kids, Nickelodeon and the Disney Channel). They feel that all their entertainment needs are met by Sky and that they have little need to revert to the terrestrial channels.

Michelle enjoys the soaps, mainly *Coronation Street*, *Emmerdale* and *EastEnders*. She watches a lot of television, particularly with the children. Michelle uses the television to pacify the children, and it is left on when the children play and when they are bathed. Michelle does not watch alone as much as John does, and family time together is scarce because of the shifts John works. Michelle says that she likes to have her "own space" at times.

The children are very demanding on the parents' time. The television, and Sky in particular, is a device or strategy to have 'family time' that is not dictated by the children and does not require the parents to provide constant attention and discipline. Were it not for the media in their home, it is hard to imagine how the family could operate as a unit. The media thus have a clear function in the Swaine household.

John likes Sky because he works shifts in a factory and there is always something good on when he gets home, whatever the time, so that he can unwind. He mainly watches television alone and can watch his choice of programmes from the extensive choice on Sky. His main viewing is sport and repeats of programmes he missed during work. He likes the fact that Sky tends to repeat the same programmes during any 24-hour period. The family rarely watches television or videos together because their work leaves little family time, and when they are together they all tend to want to watch different things.

Michelle sees 6–7 p.m. as their get-together time, while the rest of the evening is spent in conflict over who wants to watch what. It is rare for them to watch anything as a family, except for 6–7 p.m. The television, and Sky in particular, is on during the morning and when getting the children ready, but it is also on constantly in the evening, even when household members are engaged in separate activities. On one occasion it was on for the entirety of our visit of several hours, but no-one either noticed this or watched it at all. We found little use of the radio.

Both the children have televisions in their rooms and Amy has a VCR as well. She likes to have her own time and space to relax. Michelle says that the children watch television more than they play in the house, but we observed that they have considerable contact with the other children in the street and are often out of the house. John seems to spend the least amount of time engaged in collective activity, while Michelle is engaged with the children to a background of television and video most evenings.

Michelle did not know whether they received S4C or not, and when asked she proceeded to flick through the multitude of channels to find out. She said that there was "enough choice now so we don't watch it". Apparently problematically, "things on there are all Welsh". Michelle feels that she should speak Welsh, but the programmes have no interest for her. She says that her husband does not even consider himself Welsh, as his father was Irish. Indeed, she says, he hates Wales, although he was born there, because there is nothing for the children and no employment prospects.

John said that he has never watched S4C and very rarely watches BBC Wales or HTV since getting Sky. He never watches local or regional news and does not read any local or Welsh newspapers. He does not see the point of Welsh-language output because he has "never met anyone who speaks Welsh", nor has he met many who have any interest in the Welsh language – so he sees Welsh-language programming as pointless and irrelevant. In much the same vein he thought Sky was Anglocentric, but did not seem to be that bothered about this. He is happy for it to continue as it is.

John found it difficult to relate in a positive manner to Welshness. His said that Merthyr is a "bad place to live" and that he would be "out of here like a shot if I won the lottery". He admits that he and his work colleagues identify themselves as Welsh (possibly only through birth), but have very little interest in Welsh affairs, or in local news. He sees Wales as divided by the language and that there is a north-south divide between those (in the north) who think that they are the "true Welsh" and superior to his kind in the south. He feels he is typical of other men of his age in the area and that his views are in no way uncommon.

In the Swaine household the television is used as a means of entertainment that plays a background role in almost every domestic activity. Their use of Sky television seems to reflect their disassociation from and apathy towards the Welsh language and the Welsh media. In many respects they feel on the fringes of the Welsh media, neither English nor Welsh.

Chapter 3

The media

T his chapter explores the diversity of uses of each of the main mass media. It is sequenced in the order of oldest to newest, starting with the press and ending with computer games, the Internet and email. The consumption of each takes place as one activity among the multiplicity of fragmented interactions that makes up domestic life – so our account explores how the consumption of each medium is embedded in domestic routines and practices.

We examine how media consumption is changing: most obviously, television forms and viewing today are very different from the era of terrestrial-only television. At the same time, new media are arriving. In the process, some of the most interesting changes are those that occur as new media displace, complement or shape old media. The BBC website illustrates that this is not a one-way process, that old media stimulate uses of (for example) websites. The consequences of this contemporary reconfiguration are, at least potentially, very significant. At a macro level, Benedict Anderson argues that print produced the 'rational subject' and television generated 'citizenship',[32] and one might conjecture whether the new media foster the development of the 'consumer'. Our empirical evidence of media use suggests a varied and contradictory picture.

In this and subsequent chapters, the reader should be able to extend their understanding of each of the ten households, building up an increasingly elaborate picture of domestic life in each of them.

---

32 Benedict Anderson (1983) *Imagined Communities. Reflections on the Origin and Spread of Nationalism*, London, Verso.

The press

We report here our findings about the consumption of newspapers. We start by examining how newspapers arrive in a household, which members of the household choose which titles are purchased, and whether they are delivered. We then explore how members of the household use the newspaper. Like the purchasing, we found a variety of ways of reading newspapers, with a profoundly gendered patterning. We document some of the different styles of reading that we found, and link these to domestic routines in our households. We found that in some households some members made very little use of newspapers, so in these cases we explored their use of other print publications, magazines.

Investigating uses of the press was particularly difficult because the newspaper is something of a closed medium. By this we mean that reading the newspaper is an activity undertaken in closed personal space, so – rather differently from television or radio – it is difficult to see exactly which part of a newspaper is being read, or to gain any understanding of the sense that is being made of it. Reading the newspaper is a more cognitive process than is consuming most other mass media – it generally involves greater focus and is not undertaken in conjunction with other activities.

The Western Mail – a provincial morning newspaper published in Cardiff that circulates in south and west Wales – held an important place in the hearts of its readers. This loyalty was quite remarkable, as were the constructs of national identity and place that were associated with the newspaper. We discuss the meaning of *The Western Mail* for its readers in Chapter 4 (on Spaces of identification) where we discuss the relationship between *The Western Mail* and constructs of Welsh identity.

The career of the newspaper begins with its entry into the household. The Protheroes have *The Western Mail* and *The Daily Telegraph* delivered daily.

> Geoff has an annual subscription to the newspapers and therefore gets them at a cheaper price. "By subscribing, I get the Sunday editions free of charge."
> *Protheroe household, 15 September 2001*

Having the newspaper delivered is not the preferred pattern in all of our households. Several said that choice and flexibility to buy what they like, when they like, is very important.

> "We used to have it [*The Daily Post*] delivered; now I prefer to buy it when it suits me, usually in the local garage on my way home. I'll pick up a copy

> by the counter when I get petrol or milk, it's handy because it sort of reminds you that the paper's for sale ... We had it delivered up until recently, but I don't want the commitment of paying for it every day because I don't always have the time to read it every day. Buying it over the counter suits my lifestyle I suppose."
> *Julie Riley, 6 January 2002*

In the Addey and Rowlands household they seem to buy a newspaper largely because of the proximity of the paper shop.

> Paul continued to read backwards through *The Evening Post*, not really stopping anywhere. "It's a bit of a toilet read this, I only buy it out of habit and because there's a newsagent downstairs, I wouldn't have it delivered."
> *Paul Addey, 26 October 2001*

The title(s) and number of newspapers a household consumes and the means by which they obtain the newspapers reveal much about the dynamics of the household. We found clear connections between the household member who chooses which newspaper(s) the family reads, how the newspaper(s) arrive(s) and who reads the newspaper(s) first.

The Powells have *The Western Mail* delivered every day, but on Sunday they buy their newspaper from the garage or supermarket – either *The Observer* (Brian) or *The Mail on Sunday* (Rhian). Brian reads the newspaper first in the morning, because he has the time, whereas Rhian has time only after work, when she enjoys it over a coffee. Home delivery suits Brian's routine more than it does Rhian's.

> *The Western Mail* was on the kitchen table. Brian reads the 'Sports' section for the rugby and golf before going to work. He had been reading the latest news on Wales' international rugby squad and seemed puzzled and in disagreement with some of the team selection. He picked the newspaper up, but did not read it because we were talking, though he would normally use this time to have a coffee and to read it from cover to cover.
> *Powell household, 1 November 2001*

The Daniels provide an example of how taking several titles overcomes conflict over newspapers. Their wide choice leads to newspapers all over the house. Mr Daniels has stacks of old issues of national dailies and national Sundays underneath and beside the coffee table in front of the sofa where he likes to lie. Behind the sofa are a stack of books on railways and local history, as well as more old newspapers and supplements. The kitchen table is covered with the local newspapers and on one of the dining chairs there is usually a stack of colour supplements that come with the Sunday newspapers.

The Daniels have *The Sunday Times*, *The Observer* and *The Sunday Telegraph* delivered on Sunday, *The Times*, *The Western Mail* and *The Daily Mail* during the week, and the *Carmarthen Journal* delivered weekly. Mr Daniels regards *The Daily Mail* and *The Mail on Sunday* as newspapers for his wife and rarely reads them, although he sees them as good newspapers with healthy circulations. They buy the *Ammanford Guardian*, and *The Evening Post* at Tescos. The former he describes as "absolute rubbish" that he buys "out of habit". He does not really bother to read the local newspapers, and does not think much of their quality and content.
Daniels household, 20 July 2001

"I get the local paper, the *Ammanford Guardian*, for any local news of interest, although I rarely read it from cover to cover, it's more for Elizabeth to keep up to date with the local gossip."
James Daniels, 21 July 2001

Here we see in newspaper use something that Morley found regarding television news: women's preference for local news and local newspapers.[33] It is Mrs Daniels who buys *The Evening Post*.

"I'll have a look at the headlines first. It's usually Carmarthen and Swansea news, and Llanelli too. I usually keep it in the kitchen for the TV guide for the night and the following day. I don't know why I buy it really, there's not that much in it. I suppose I just like to keep up with what's going on locally."
Mrs Daniels, 1 December 2001

It is not just the choice of newspaper that is gendered. How newspapers are used also reflects the division of labour in the household.

Mrs Daniels spent much of the day preparing the Sunday lunch. She had been up to the farm to check on the new fences, while Mr Daniels had been there very early that morning for a walk. Since returning, Mr Daniels had remained in the living room reading the newspaper with Classic FM on in the background. Mr Daniels had been reading the headlines from *The Sunday Times* and *The Sunday Telegraph* that day, along with the business and television supplements. He spent a long time reading *The*

---

33 David Morley (1992) *Television Audiences and Cultural Studies*, London, Routledge.

Sunday Times supplement on education and university league tables. John flicked through the 'Culture' supplement of *The Sunday Times* and the television listings from the *Telegraph*. Mrs Daniels occasionally sat down and had a look through the *You* magazine from *The Mail on Sunday* and read a feature about the BBC's *Ground Force* team. This was for a short period, around ten minutes, then she returned to the kitchen to look after the lunch.

Daniels household, 20 July 2001

Mrs Daniels glanced quickly at *You* magazine from *The Mail on Sunday* then carried on in the kitchen. "I don't get much time to read anything from start to finish, every time I start to get into something good, the phone rings, or someone calls around … I like the travel features and the articles from around the world." Whereas Sunday is Mr Daniels' day without work, for Mrs Daniels it is the busiest day – with the whole household plus visitors around.

Mrs Daniels, 23 September 2001

Thus we see that women read different newspapers, and in different places. Rhian Powell, unlike her son and husband, reads the newspaper in the kitchen.

"If the boys are watching something in the living room, I'll be in the kitchen reading the paper … I like to keep the listings near the portable in the kitchen."

Rhian Powell, 1 November 2001

The Rileys share space, but provide another example of the gendered use of the newspaper, on this occasion in the kitchen on a Sunday.

I arrived as the couple sat in the kitchen having a late breakfast. They both sat at the small kitchen table. I entered through the back door, which is clear and double-glazed and gives the kitchen an open light almost like a conservatory. I was offered a cup of tea. *The Observer* was on the table, Julie Riley had the magazine and Richard the broadsheet section. Julie had reached the section where there are book and theatre reviews, along with audio CD, DVD and video reviews.

Richard was reading the headline about the critical condition of the chancellor's daughter. He commented: "How terrible they must feel, you can't imagine can you, it's the worst thing that could ever happen to a parent … I hope the media leave them alone, it must be terrible being in the public eye at this time."

Richard continued on to the inner pages, seemingly scanning the news as he flicked through. "It says here that interest rates are probably going to go up because people are over-spending, especially over Christmas."

Julie said to me, "He likes to tell me the news, it's not like I can't read it for myself. I don't need to, he does it for me. You would have made a good news presenter you know … He reads the newspaper in the morning, so I don't need to later on, it's more his thing, I don't have the time on a Sunday to sit and read it. I'll have the supplement in the morning and I've usually finished with it by the end of the night. I'll read a bit now and some later in front of the television. There's usually not that much on and I'll read with one eye on the screen if something catches my eye. The evening's more my time to relax."
Riley household, 6 January 2002

The James household is unique among our ten households in that the choice of newspaper is governed by the mother, who tends to be the main reader of newspapers in the household. She buys *The Daily Post* from the local shop. On the days she does not work, she might pick up the newspaper before midday, and on her working days she buys it later and reads it in the evening. She is the one who chooses and buys the Sunday newspaper (*The Mail on Sunday*), too, and is the first to read it.

"Well I pick them up from the shop, Ieuan doesn't really read the papers that much, he prefers the news on television … When it comes to the news, I like to have the papers. You get a bit sick of watching the television all the time, and it's nice to read the news I think."
Lucy James, 7 January 2002

They do not take a national daily newspaper because other members of the household prefer BBC News 24 or Sky News. Lucy sees the local paper and terrestrial television as her thing. She reads *The Daily Post* most days, for the local news and obituaries, and at the weekend browses *The Mail on Sunday* magazines after she has dissected the main newspaper for articles of interest.

I arrived at the house at 6 p.m. on a Sunday night. The whole family had been together for lunch and were now winding down for the evening. The cold weather had put paid to some of the boys' outdoor activities and they had chosen to stay in. Lucy was sitting in an armchair looking through Saturday's edition of *The Daily Post* to scan the television listings of terrestrial channels for that night. She also had *The Mail on Sunday* by her

feet, open at the holiday section near the back. She said she had been reading off and on before I arrived. The two newspapers by her suggested that the newspapers were her pleasure on a Sunday afternoon.
James household, 7 January 2002

Lucy James does not bother with the business or sports pages at all. Other members of the family read the newspaper after she has finished.

> "The paper is in a hell of a mess afterwards, we spend the rest of the day putting the paper back into order and ironing the pages."
> *Ieuan James, 29 August 2001*

Karen Lewis's boys read *The Western Mail* after her – she leaves it on the table for them. They start with the sports pages – because they both have an active interest in rugby and football, supporting Swansea teams in both. Dafydd, the older son, sometimes reads the business pages to help him with his 'A' level Economics. After the sport (and for Dafydd the business) they read the front page headlines, then read it in page order.

Exploring the reasons for buying different newspapers, we compared the local press with national newspapers.

> Stuart Chandler is an example of someone who does not buy a local or national newspaper, but reads the newspapers as part of his job, the *Carmarthen Journal, Western Telegraph* and *Tivy-Side Advertiser*. These are circulated so that members of the office can contribute to the newspapers' weekly farmers' update. Part of Stuart's job is to assist in writing this small column, which is printed in these newspapers each week. He sometimes takes a newspaper home to have a quick look through.
> *Chandler and Thomas household, 21 June 2001*

In the course of our research Stuart started buying *The Western Mail* on Thursdays and the *South Wales Post* on Wednesdays, because he was looking for a new job. He thinks *The Western Mail* and *The Carmarthen Journal* have the better vacancies but that the jobs in these are a bit out of his league, so sees *The Evening Post* as the best chance of a new job. Generally, however, he said that he "couldn't be bothered" to read a newspaper, especially for national and international news – for which he prefers to keep up-to-date with Sky or HTV news.

Nicola Davies has very little interest in newspapers, and no intention of buying one, local or national. She is happy to pick up and flick through her father's newspapers. Referring to the *South Wales Echo* she said:

"I'll read my stars and have a look what's on the television for the night. My Dad buys *The Welsh Mirror*, I'll have a look at that as well for the stars and the gossip, you know! ... I sometimes look at the job adverts if I've had a bad day in work."
Nicola Davies, 24 September 2001

Paul Addey reads the local newspaper for news of his local soccer team and for a column on local music.

Paul said that he was going to pick up a newspaper from the shop later on. He usually buys *The Evening Post* during the week for a quick look at local events. He buys it for the local gig listings and 'Spiv's column', a regular local commentary by a small local celebrity called Spiv. "The guy hasn't got a clue", but Paul looks forward to a mention of his own band and comments on gigs that they've played in the column. *The Evening Post* provides a small platform for local musicians to make a name for themselves on the local scene. The column appears every Friday and includes gig guides, record and gig reviews, music news and occasional photos of local bands, and this was one reason to buy the newspaper. Christopher reads this column too, to keep up with the local scene.
Addey and Rowlands household, 26 June 2001

Richard and Judy were still on the television as the two eat their snack. Paul eat while also reading *The Evening Post*, while Anna (Paul's girlfriend) watched the television. Christopher picked up *The Welsh Mirror* briefly and glanced at the headlines. Paul offered me a cup of tea, we sat down and Paul smoked a cigarette. He bent over the newspaper, roll-up cigarette in one hand and tea in the other. We talked yet again about sport, Welsh rugby and Swansea City in particular. Paul had picked up *The Evening Post* for coverage of Swansea City's supporters' protest over a hostile take-over. Paul seemed concerned for the future of the club.
Addey and Rowlands household, 23 October 2001

We found that local newspapers were sometimes bought for specific reasons, such as local sport, employment and local news and events, and not read in any depth, but on a 'pick and flick' basis.[34] This is exemplified by Karen Lewis's use of her local weekly newspaper.

---

[34] Mark Pursehouse identifies 'flicking' as a style of reading *The Sun*. See M. Pursehouse (1991) 'Looking at "*The Sun*": into the nineties with a tabloid and its readers', *Cultural Studies From Birmingham Vol. 1*.

I decided to help Karen with her work around the house. She had told me about a block in her guttering, so I got a ladder to clear it for her. She popped out to the corner shop, four doors up the road. She returned with Hannah, with an assortment of treats for her for later on that day. She had also bought me a can of Pepsi for my efforts. She had decided to buy a newspaper in the shop. The *Brecon and Radnor Chronicle* is delivered free, but Karen had paid 30p for the *Brecon and Radnor Express*, a local weekly. I stood half-way up the ladder, clearing the silt and leaves from the guttering. From the window, I could see Karen and Hannah sitting by the dining table. Hannah was playing with a Barbie with half her hair pulled out, while Karen flicked through the local newspaper, reading some of the reports of the local play and the back page to see if there was a picture of Dafydd in the school rugby team that had won the regional final in a schools competition. She had bought it to see pictures of the community play. The play had made the national news of Wales, as a rural, post foot and mouth story. Karen told me, "I helped sew the costumes for the play, most of the town were involved in some way. It's got some photographs in the centre, so we'll keep them. Hannah was one of the sheep in the last scene."
Karen Lewis, 20 January 2002

Several of our research subjects made connections between newspaper reporting and local life. The crime reports in the *Echo* are invoked by Nicola Davies as a rationale for not going out in Cardiff. Angharad Protheroe, too, sees Cardiff as a place to avoid at night because of the reported street violence. Mrs Daniels sees Ammanford as a changed place because of the drug-related incidents and deaths that she reads about in the *Ammanford Guardian* and *The Evening Post*.

Regional and national newspapers offer a broader range of topics, news and articles than local newspapers, and often come with supplements – hence they are read for longer than are local newspapers. The Powells read *The Western Mail* for its range of news.

"It's not a bad read, it's as good as any of the other broadsheets and it's focused on Wales. It's a better paper than it used to be, it's not as old-fashioned, it's got a better layout, the sport's better and the business and motoring supplements are a good read."
Brian Powell, 1 November 2001

"I usually keep up-to-date with current affairs by reading *The Daily Mail* or *The Western Mail* in the house. Someone's usually got a paper in work.

I'll read that over a coffee."
Rhian Powell, 1 November 2001

Karen Lewis reads *The Western Mail* headlines at work, and reads it from cover to cover when she gets home. She tends to read it over dinner, avoiding the sports and business sections. She feels that it has "a masculine feel" but that it caters well for women in Wales, and that it has improved in this respect over the past few years.

Richard Riley has *The Observer* delivered so that he can read a whole range of news and lifestyle articles, in which he has taken a greater interest since retiring.

> *The Observer* was on the kitchen table, it had been delivered earlier. "I've only had a quick look at it, I normally scan the headlines, the centre pages are running a story on possible economic slowdown before Christmas and the rise in house prices ... I'm more interested in how all these interest rates are going to kill my savings. We own our house now, but it's a great time to borrow ... We like the travel supplements and the culture supplements; it gives you ideas for holidays in places you've never been before. I really like the gardening features, you get some nice tips." Richard moved around the kitchen putting all the vegetables to boil. "I don't mind cooking actually, I think it's since I started to watch *Ready Steady Cook*, it's given me some great ideas. Food is the new fashion." Turning to *The Observer*, he comments, "Look, there are always features about cooking and fusion foods. It's trendy to cook, especially for men. My Dad couldn't boil a pan of water."
> *Richard Riley, 6 November 2001*

Mrs Daniels tends to go for lifestyle sections when she has time to read the newspaper.

> I'm into planting flowers and gardening in general, so I'm always looking for any tips on growing tomatoes and different seasonal plants for around the farm. They've always got good cake recipes as well, I often give them a go from the back of *You* magazine.
> *Elizabeth Daniels, 1 December 2001*

The amount a newspaper is read is, in part, a function of the time available. Karen Lewis works and is a single parent with three children, and her consumption of the newspaper reflects the hectic nature of her life.

> "To buy and read a Sunday newspaper is a rare treat. I don't have much

time to read the paper at home, on Sunday I'll maybe get an hour to read it after food. I'll buy it because I can keep the supplements and read them during the following week. I hardly read the paper from cover to cover, I skip through for interesting news, with the supplements they've got a more general feel and I can read them anytime ... Usually I'll have about twenty minutes to read it between 6 and 7 at night, that's when all the kids are doing something and they've all had food. The newspapers are a luxury, I can't make time to read them, I'll just skip through them when I can."
Karen Lewis, 20 September 2001

The Protheroes, by contrast, are retired empty-nesters, and their use of the newspaper is very different; they have much more time and are under less pressure. Reading the newspaper is a form of relaxation in the privacy of their home.

"I read the paper in the kitchen, usually in the afternoon when I get home from dinners at the school. Geoff reads them both in the morning and again around teatime. We both read *The Western Mail*, he reads *The Daily Telegraph* as well. We have them delivered every day, but *The Western Mail* does not come out on a Sunday. I split my time between the kitchen and the conservatory, I relax in both rooms I suppose, I enjoy cooking and I like to sit and look at the view from the conservatory, that's better than television any day. I'll read the paper in the conservatory mostly, over a cup of something. Sunday, I enjoy a good read in the morning, I take a look at the papers, but I prefer a book to be honest, although I'll read it after Geoff."
Angharad Protheroe, 12 December 2001

The Swaine household has children, and both parents work. John Swaine works shifts and he uses the newspaper as a means of passing the time at work.[35] He illustrates the shared use of the newspaper at work.

"I'll take the paper to work. I can read it in my breaks. It just passes the time in work, you can switch off from the rest of the factory ... I normally just read the sport first and then the rest of it. Most of the time someone else will read it in work after me, but it always comes home with me."
John Swaine, 25 January 2002

35 Mark Pursehouse found that *The Sun* was read at work by men, but not women, and used at lunch and tea breaks, as a means of marking time. See M. Pursehouse (1991) 'Looking at "*The Sun*": into the nineties with a tabloid and its readers', *Cultural Studies from Birmingham*, vol. 1.

The Swaines have a system whereby they swap newspapers with Michelle's parents most days. They buy *The Sun*, and her father buys *The Welsh Mirror*. The grandparents drop the children off from school and swap the newspapers every day, except when John is working an afternoon shift. Both households benefit from the system in that they get two newspapers for the price of one.

Mrs Daniels shows how long a newspaper can circulate in a household – because the tabloid or general interest sections date less quickly. Thus the career of the newspaper can last much longer than the cover date.

> "I usually read the *You* section of *The Mail on Sunday*. I'll read it and some of the papers late on Sunday after dinner. We have too many papers delivered and they're always spread around the house for the rest of the week. We've got piles of newspapers in the living room going way back. I sometimes find myself reading the supplements during the week, they're quite a good read over a coffee. I just flick through them really."
> *Elizabeth Daniels, 23 August 2001*

In households where we found little or no use of newspapers, we examined the use of magazines. Christopher Rowlands said that he would never buy the local or national newspapers, but he spends a considerable amount on lifestyle, film and games console magazines.

> Christopher leaves his film and music journals (*Empire* and *Mojo*) in the bathroom, along with *Dreamcast* magazine. Many back issues lie around on the floor of the bathroom and are picked up and read when the lads are in there.
> *Addey and Rowlands household, 17 June 2001*

Empire, *Mojo*, *Q* and *NME* reflect and inform his taste in film and music. They allow him to distinguish himself as a discerning music fan, to appear well-informed when talking with friends about recent releases, and to make an informed choice about the products on the market.

Mrs Daniels has the *Smallholder* magazine delivered monthly, and her son John reads the biker press to inform him of events and rallies. He identifies with these biker magazines, which he sees as representing his lifestyle. For him, they are like newspapers, in that they reflect and sustain his identity and inform his social routines.

> The garage was full of old spare parts and the carcasses of several abandoned bikes. The cassette radio in the garage was spluttering out Lynyrd Skynyrd (a 1970s rock band) and John was in the process of

adjusting one of the brake discs. He told me that he is one of a small number of Harley Davidson enthusiasts in this part of the country, and he travels regularly around the UK to meet other owners at organised events. These events are publicised in national bike magazines such as *Back Street Heroes* (BSH) and *Motor Cycle News* (MCN). John has these publications ordered at the newsagent down the road. BSH comes out every month, while MCN is published weekly. The magazines provide John with news of forthcoming events, discount accessories and product reviews. He tends to read MCN for the mechanical and performance related items. BSH is more about the biker lifestyle, reporting rallies, forthcoming bike festivals, music (mostly rock and blues), and bands and gigs around the country – it is a magazine by bikers, for bikers.
John Daniels, 20 July 2001

Dafydd Lewis also does not read a newspaper, but he buys into a club culture, as represented in magazines, even though this is a culture from which he is distanced in real life.

Dafydd occasionally buys *Loaded* for its light-hearted lifestyle content and *Mixmag* for its clubbing culture. Dafydd likes these magazines for their focus on club music and their appeal to young men. He likes the lifestyle aspect of *Mixmag* and would like to go on holiday to Ibiza very soon. He is keen on dance music and the magazines inform him of the latest hot clubs and the best new music releases. Living in Builth Wells, however, means that he never gets to attend any of these events because he spends weekends working at his Dad's farm and going out drinking in Builth.
Dafydd Lewis, 6 September 2001

While her husband and son were watching *Top Gear* in the living room, Rhian Powell had a coffee in the kitchen and explained her magazine purchasing.

She buys *Chat* magazine from a newsagent near her place of work. She buys it while she is out buying a sandwich or something for lunch. "It's a coffee read, I buy it sometimes, and only because I usually get a sandwich from the newsagent near the office. It's full of stupid stories really, it's like bubble gum for the brain, isn't it?"
Rhian Powell, 1 November 2001

This illustrates how, as other research has found, most magazines (like much radio, television and the press) assume a quite limited and discontinuous degree of concentration in their audiences or readerships; they are 'put-downable'.[36]

At the specialist end of the spectrum of magazines, Stuart Chandler buys *Warhammer* and *White Dwarf*, each £3.50 monthly. These are an integral part of his fantasy role-play games: he buys and paints intricate models which represent characters in game books. The magazines include extensions of current games and new story lines and quests, which form the basis of the games. He plays about once a week with friends from Ammanford, and there are games workshops in Swansea as well as national and international tournaments. The magazines sustain and inform both the skill of model-making and the competition of game-playing.

Generally, however, the growth of lifestyle supplements blurs the boundary between newspapers and magazines, and means that both are used in similar ways and for similar purposes.

To conclude, we found that newspapers in our households enjoyed varied careers. This was characterised by gender differences, with men much more likely to choose whether it is delivered, women more likely to read local newspapers, and men more likely to prefer a national newspaper, and to read the newspaper first. Styles of reading newspapers relate to gender, age and lifestyle, with the level of engagement with the newspaper depending significantly on the amount of time available. Most local newspapers are bought from nearby outlets and are bought for television guides, local employment, sport and out of a general curiosity for local news. Nationals are bought for current affairs, but also for their lifestyle supplements. The Sunday nationals have a broad appeal because of their wide range of features and their longevity of use. Some of our respondents showed little enthusiasm for newspapers, but regularly bought lifestyle and special-interest magazines, which are used for similar purposes to newspapers.

Radio

We documented when and where the radio is listened to, and examined the connections between the uses of radio and household routines. All of our households had at least one radio, and we begin by examining how listening to the radio slots into domestic routines – particularly in the morning, in the kitchen. Next we discuss different styles or modes of listening, each of which involves a different level of attention to the broadcast. Most radio listening involves using the radio as background, though there is a style of listening that involves serious, uninterrupted attention being given to a programme – but this is very rare. Using

36 Joke Hermes (1995) *Reading Women's Magazines: An Analysis of Everyday Media Use*, Cambridge, Polity Press, p. 32.

the radio as background varies between almost not listening, carefully selecting a programme to accompany some other activity, and (most actively) using the radio to set the mood for some other activity, to create a soundscape or ambience. Finally, we examine how multi-channel cable and satellite are both a threat and an opportunity for radio: we found that music television has replaced radio as a source of background music in some households, while in other households we found that radio by Sky means greater use of radio.

Many of our households listen to very little radio, and radio listening constitutes a very low proportion of the time spent engaged with the media in the home. In nearly all of our households, however, someone listens to regular radio shows or presenters. They mainly tune in to one presenter and certainly one station, either in the morning or at weekends, with a strong loyalty. Radio provides another voice, company in the background and a means to fill household space with sound. In this context radio has an advantage over audio CDs and tapes – in that it involves a personality, that is transmitted to the listener, allowing mediated communication or company and communicating the feeling that the listener is being spoken to as an individual.[37] Radio is seldom used outside patterned times that fit around household rituals and routines such as breakfast, washing up and cleaning.[38] Of the mass media, radio is perhaps the most background one. It is low-key and general, with repetition of messages the major source of its impact; 'consumption is apparently vast but its impact minor'.[39] With radio the listener does not have to give their full attention, it fits into life without requiring full attention; listeners can connect without engagement or commitment.

In most of our households the radio is listened to primarily in the morning over breakfast, in the car on the way to work and on weekend mornings. Radio use in the kitchen provides the backdrop for what in most households is a busy morning routine. People have too little time to look up at a television or to concentrate on reading. The radio provides aural stimulation, while allowing individuals to free their eyes and hands for other things. The James household in Bangor is typical in this respect, demonstrating what has been called an 'informational' repertoire of listening.[40]

---

37 There is an interesting body of literature on broadcasting's 'mode of address'. See Martin Montgomery (1986) 'DJ talk', *Media, Culture & Society*, vol. 8, pp. 421–440; and Paddy Scannell (1991) *Broadcast Talk*, London, Sage. The Henley Centre (1993) found that 63 per cent of radio listeners listen alone. See Henley Centre (1993) *Media Futures*, London, Henley Centre.

38 Paddy Scannell describes radio's appeal, function and relevance in terms of its 'dailiness', its integration with the dynamics and rhythms of everyday life. See P. Scannell (1996) *Radio, Television and Modern Life: A Phenomenological Approach*, Oxford, Blackwell.

39 Andrew Crisell (1986) *Understanding Radio*, London, Methuen, p. 191.

I woke up at 7 a.m., the same time as the rest of the family. Lucy laid out a variety of cereals on the table and members of the family each took a bowl from the kitchen. She also made toast. Ieuan switched the radio on to listen to *Post Cyntaf* (on Radio Cymru) at about 7.30 a.m.

"Dwi'n gwrando ar hwn bob dydd .... Hwn 'dy'r unig beth dwi'n cael yn rheolaidd .... Fi yw'r cyntaf i adael yn y bore i'r gwaith a mae Radio Cymru yn aros ar yn y car am y siwrne ugain munud i'r ysgol." ["I listen to this every day ... it's the only thing I suppose I really have as a routine each day ... I'm the first to leave in the morning for work and Radio Cymru stays on in the car for the twenty minute journey to school."]

After Ieuan had gone to work, Gwyn turned on BBC1 for the morning news and headlines.

"Fel arfer mae o ar tan 8.30, wedyn wnai wylio Discovery am awr. Fedra i ddim heddiw achos rwy'n mynd i lawr i'r Trallwng i helpu 'mrawd efo'i blannu." ["Usually it's on until about 8.30, then I'll watch Discovery for an hour. I can't today 'cos I'm going down to my brother's in Welshpool to help him out with some planting."]

Lucy still had the radio on in the kitchen as she cleaned up. She does not speak Welsh, but the radio was still tuned to Radio Cymru. I asked her whether she was listening to it.

"I pick out the odd word, I'm not really paying any attention at this time in the morning, I'm just getting everything in place ready to go ... I'll switch it off when the dishes are away ... I'll dry the dishes, switch off the radio, the light and I'm away through the door."
Lucy James, 8 January 2002

Thus we see the radio as background and as a part of a routine – heard rather than listened to, as an accompaniment to everyday life, and for a time-span that does not correspond with the duration of the programme. In the Davies household, the radio provides the kick-start the morning needs, providing mediated company.

There is a CD radio cassette player in the small kitchen, which has a small pile of CD singles next to it. Nicola tells me that she listens to Radio One's breakfast show with Sarah Cox and sings along with the songs she likes.

40 Susan Douglas (1999) *Listening In: Radio and the American Imagination, from Amos 'n' Andy and Edward R. Murrow to Wolfman Jack and Howard Stern*, New York and Toronto, Random House.

"I like Radio One in the morning, she [Cox] plays all the stuff I like and she's quite funny. I think she's all right actually, there's loads of music, I hate it when they just talk all the time, you can't sing along. It definitely wakes me up in the morning."
Nicola Davies, 24 September 2001

The Powell household shows how the radio is a medium that flows with members' activities during the busy morning period. The radio carries over from the kitchen to the car. It suits the context of consumption in that it requires the individual only to listen. The radio is used as a background while people engage in other tasks.

Brian usually gives Gareth a lift to school on his way to the practice, and often has to keep shouting up the stairs for Gareth to get out of bed in time. Gareth comes to the kitchen in time to grab an assortment of crisps and fruit from the kitchen to eat on his way to school. Occasionally he will have time for cereal, but very rarely. Gareth put his CD personal stereo and a mobile in his bag – for shutting out his father's choice of radio programme and his outbursts toward other road users while in the car.

"I listen to the stereo in the car if he's got Roy Noble on or something. I listen to it when I'm walking home mostly, but it comes in handy if he's going on about the traffic."
Gareth Powell, 8 January 2002

Though largely confined to the morning, radio is, of course, listened to at other times of the day.

The Lewis family listen to both Radio One and Radio Cymru most evenings. The boys like to listen to the *Chris Moyles* show on Radio One when they get home from school. Karen listens to Radio Cymru in the morning before work while having breakfast and sometimes at night. She tuned in daily recently to hear coverage of the National Eisteddfod. The boys listen to the radio at weekend in the tractor if they are working, usually Radio One, or Radio Cymru if their father is there because he can't stand Radio One.
Lewis household, 14 September 2001

Radio is used to fill the space, to act as a background to regular household activities. Often the listener will not even be aware that it is on, or will not give it sufficient attention to remember what they have listened to. Karen Lewis listens to the radio most morning and evenings, but her recollection of what she listens to is poor – a case of listening but not hearing. This demonstrates how the radio becomes lost in the background of a busy household, not really grabbing the attention of the listener for much of the time that it is being used.

> Karen said that she usually listened to the radio in the kitchen, usually switching between Radio Cymru and Radio One, "depending on who's in the room at the time". She said that she does not really know what she listens to. Usually it is just on in the background when she is cooking or doing something with the children. "I'll switch between the stations if there's too much chatter and not enough music. If I want a specific song I'll put a CD on sometimes."
> *Karen Lewis, 20 September 2001*

Radio becomes part of the kitchen routine. Switching on the radio in the morning becomes like switching on the kettle or the light switch. Its association with the kitchen means that it is a largely forgotten medium elsewhere in the household. Use becomes habitual, automatic and unfocused.

Having said that, it is not only in the kitchen that the radio is used as background for other activities, filling space.

> "I get things done a lot quicker with some music in the background. I've got some cleaning and hoovering to do, so it takes my mind off it ... who needs aerobics when you've got a house this size to keep clean and two hulks who don't lift a finger in the week. The radio's mainly for background when I'm too busy to read or sit down, so I suppose the radio's my main thing."
> *Karen Lewis, 20 September 2001*

For his rather more relaxed activity, Richard Riley has a radio in the shed, tuned to Classic FM.

As well as radio as a backdrop to busy times, we found a more selective form of listening, with individuals tuning in routinely to a specific programme or personality. The main motivation is the radio personality and the mediated company this provides during breaks or quiet times in the day. Others have explained the mass appeal of radio in terms of its unique relationship with the listener, its capacity to address or 'speak' to the individual in a personal, almost intimate, way. This is radio as background, but for less-rushed, more laid-back, peaceful moments. It involves simultaneous activity, but more engagement with the broadcast. Sometimes when reading the newspaper, Richard Riley likes to have discussion programmes on Radio Four on in the background.

He tells me that it's like in the staff room in work: you can listen to other people's voices, but keep your own counsel at the same time.
Riley household, 6 November 2001

Rhian Powell told us about her use of radio.

"Saturday and Sunday mornings, I love to listen to Radio Wales over breakfast. We usually get the papers out as well. *Money for Nothing* with Owen Money is on Saturday and *A String of Pearls* on Sunday. They're probably the best things on Radio Wales, apart from Roy Noble in the week. I'll listen to him in the car if I'm travelling with work, or if I've got a day off and I'm doing something around the house."
Rhian Powell, 1 November 2001

Like other listeners to specific shows, Brian Powell feels some kind of connection with the presenter. Roy Noble on Radio Wales has a light-hearted tone and an accent and mode of address that resonates with Brian's world view. The mediated company provides a backdrop for his relatively sedate afternoon.

"I like Roy, he's a man of the people, we often listen to him on our days off or in the car, it's a good mix of music, comedy and chat, it's easy background listening ... I was just reading, I've got some time off and I'm going to play golf later. It's ideal, the house is empty and I can put my feet up. I can read and listen to the radio at the same time. It's perfect."
Brian Powell, 8 January 2002

"On Sundays I'll listen to Classic FM and Radio Cymru in the morning when I read the papers."
Mr Daniels, 20 July 2001

The Powells affiliation with Radio Wales represents an identification with a geographically based community. But there is also at play an 'associational' form of viewing – when music is associated in our minds with a particular event, place or period in our lives.[41]

The next kind of listening we identified is when the radio is still on in the background, but is used to create the ambience for an activity. Radio becomes a means to alter or create a soundscape, mood or ambience. This is a more proactive use of the radio, than simply background. The notion of 'soundscape' allows us to understand the link between location of use and mood. We found

---

41   Susan Douglas (1999) *Listening In: Radio and the American Imagination, from Amos 'n' Andy and Edward R. Murrow to Wolfman Jack and Howard Stern*, New York and Toronto, Random House.

some who use the radio (and other audio devices) with headphones, to create personal space for the consumption of sound. Others use it to create the ambience for the activity in which they are engaged.

At the more passive end of the spectrum, Christopher Rowlands likes the ambience and feel of the radio.

"I do like to have television or radio on when I'm in the house alone, because it tends to fill the room, its nice to have it on because it gives an atmosphere, it's surprising with the radio what you take in, you don't necessarily sit there and listen to it, but I'll have Radio Two on a lot."
Chris Rowlands, 19 June 2001

In a more engaged way, Richard Riley enjoys the sounds of Classic FM, as he gets inspired to do the cooking.

Richard had begun to enjoy cooking since he retired; he looked quite at home in the kitchen and had Classic FM on in the background providing the musical inspiration for the food. His stirring and chopping seemed to go in rhythm with the music. The kitchen was full of life, with the music, the dog and Richard orchestrating the whole affair. I did not know that cooking could be so involved!
Riley household, 6 November 2001

In Mrs Daniels' stables, the radio brings the horsewomen together in song.

I was helping out around the stables and found myself talked into a number of tasks involving wheelbarrows and horse manure. The work was light-ened by the sounds of *Steve Wright* on Radio Two playing *Love Me Do* by The Beatles in the background. Elizabeth, Helen and Angharad occasion-ally augment this with bursts of song from their respective stables.
Daniels household, 20 July 2001

The main radio stations listened to in our households were UK national radio, but we found one case of the use of independent local radio for specialist programming. This case was a relatively active form of engagement with the broadcast.

"Radio One is full of manufactured bands, but Radio Two is surprisingly good because they've got more of a free rein to do what they want. That's where, if you're going to hear anything exciting, that's where it'll be. Red Dragon is surprisingly good, they'll play a lot of unsigned bands, you know most bands round here could get on there, but it's a good thing. The radio

raises the profile of unsigned bands and makes people take them more seriously, people tend to think if you haven't got a record deal then you're no good, that's just not the case."
Christopher Rowlands, 19 June 2001

Here we see a generational sense of community – a sense of community in that the isolated listener is very much aware of other isolated listeners.[42] Christopher saw Swansea Sound and The Wave as less good than Red Dragon for his taste in music, but good for Swansea because they promoted events and gigs in Singleton Park and Morfa Stadium, providing live shows and festival-like environments for young people in Swansea.

Stuart Chandler uses the radio when he is painting his small die-cast warhammer figures in the kitchen. He enjoys the odd occasion when he gets the flat to himself, and when he does he uses the radio quite intensively to transcend the confines of his living room. This shows a rather different use of the radio from that which we observed elsewhere, and it is in itself a rare occurrence, even in this household. It might be characterised as a male style of listening.

> Stuart was alone for the evening, as Ann had been called away to visit her sisters in Ystalefera. Stuart was listening to Radio Four when I arrived, sitting in his armchair, listening to the original radio version of *The Hitch-Hikers Guide to the Galaxy*, which was being re-broadcast. Stuart and I sat with a coffee listening. It was the episode where the secret of the universe is revealed as the number 42. I arrived during the last quarter of the show, which seemed to put Stuart off the enjoyment he had been having on his own. We talked, but not much, until the show was over.
> *Stuart Chandler, 24 October 2001*

Perhaps most interesting is the emergence of music video television and digital radio. In some households, we were told of a reduced use of the radio (local and national) in favour of music video, or more distant stations. We did not come across any use of Internet radio in our research, but we did encounter the use of radio via Sky.[43]

> At around 10.30 I went into the living room, where Brian was lying across the sofa reading a book he had received for Christmas. In the background,

---

42   As Dorothy Hobson found. See D. Hobson (1980) 'Housewives and the mass media' in Stuart Hall *et al.* (eds) *Culture, Media, Language: Working Papers in Cultural Studies 1972–79*, London, Hutchinson.

43   RAJAR recently found that 20 per cent of people report that they have listened to radio via their television sets. See 'Digital kills the Radio 1 stars', *Media Guardian*, 4 August 2003, p. 4.

he was listening to Roy Noble's morning show. Brian was tuned into Radio Wales – listening to digital radio via satellite television. The show was on only briefly, and at this point consisted of telephone requests, with Roy engaged in conversation with members of his audience.

"I suppose I did flick through for a while, there's certainly a lot of choice and specialist stuff, I'm more of a fan of a good host, a personality who entertains as well as plays some music that I can listen to. Most of the stuff is not really my cup of tea; I prefer a talk show with some hits from the sixties thrown in ... we like Owen Money's show as well ... I suppose I started to listen to some other channels out of curiosity really, again you don't have the trouble of tuning in to find the station, they're all pre-set on Sky so it's as easy as switching channels ... you haven't got to endure all that interference while you're searching for the channel you want, it's a lot better."
Brain Powell, 28 December 2001

Radio as a device for providing music in the home is thus challenged by Sky and cable television. Using the television set to listen to radio changes the uses of household spaces such as the kitchen, centralising media consumption on the television set and the living room. More than this, in some instances radio by cable or satellite seems to be replacing television viewing, as well as extending radio listening.

"I discovered the radio channels ages ago, if there's nothing else on, I'll listen to Radio Wales anyway, it's just as easy to switch it on through the TV. In fact, it's a better reception and I don't have to manually tune to it, I just select the channel from the menu and there it is ... it's really simple actually and, as I say, with digital the reception of the station is usually a bit clearer than in the kitchen. I tend to flick between the radio and the TV sometimes if there's nothing on. I wouldn't have bothered with the radio before, because it meant switching something else on, or going to another room. It's all in one place with me now, so I use it more if anything."
Brian Powell, 28 December 2001

Radio competes with audiotapes and CDs for creating soundscapes in the household, while music video channels on television pose a threat to both radio and CDs as forms of aural consumption. Paul Addey told us that his radio hi-fi was not working, but that he hardly ever listened to it anyway.

"I still watch a lot of MTV2 or VH1 on television, but the radio on my stereo

doesn't work anymore, I don't listen to a lot of radio anyway, mostly CDs … MTV is good because they showcase a lot of bands you might not hear on the radio. If I like a song and I hear it often enough, then I'm more likely to buy it. Saying that, I'm probably just as likely to copy it from someone else, or get someone to download it from the Internet for me."
Paul Addey, 16 October 2001

For the Swaines, too, television has made the radio almost obsolete and has led to a reduction in the buying of recorded music.

"We don't bother with the radio at all any more, we've got about 16 channels of music on Sky, I think it's 16 maybe 14, but the kids listen to the Smash Hits channel a lot, John will listen to VH1 and MTV."
Michelle Swaine, 23 October 2001

"I don't bother [with the radio], there's enough music on the television that covers my taste. I listen to the *Classic Hour* on VH1, mostly 80s stuff, not classical music. We've got all these music channels and radio stations in our package, so I don't really see the need to put the radio on, or go out and buy a record. I've got my collection upstairs, but I haven't bought anything new for ages."
John Swaine, 23 October 2001

We found that the radio is the most easy-to-use background media, and was used during the busiest times, and in the busiest places, in our households. For most, the kitchen has become synonymous with the use of the radio. Radio use is largely confined to breakfast time and the kitchen. Radio is enjoyed as a form of mediated company, with individuals tuning in to hear specific presenters and shows. Its main use, however, is as background – ranging from background sound that is hardly listened to, to the active creation of soundscapes, generally as an accompaniment to everyday life, listened to while doing other things. One of its great strengths is that radio can be consumed without using one's eyes or hands. Music television provides the latest challenge to the radio, as well as to audiotapes and CDs, while radio by cable or satellite provides a new way of using an old medium, easily accessed and in the living room.

Television

In this section we report on the consumption of television, VCRs and teletext. Our focus is on multi-channel television, and various new developments that we found to be associated with this. We begin by discussing the very mundane nature of most television viewing. Some viewing, however, is quite the opposite, with particular programmes really important in some people's lives. We examine how VCRs are used, allowing greater consumer control of broadcasting. Like VCRs, multiple sets and fragmented viewing in households enhance choice and control – in this case spatially rather than the temporal shift allowed by the VCR. From bedroom and kitchen viewing we move to the living room. We discuss the re-emergence of the television as hearth – with the arrival of multimedia home entertainment systems and devices. These new home entertainment systems are important not just in themselves, but also for their impact on uses of traditional media technologies, notably the VCR and (as we have discussed in Chapter 3) the radio. We describe the various styles of viewing that we encountered, particularly in multi-channel households, and note the profound differences in how (as well as where) television is viewed by men and women, and in the attention each are able to give to a programme. Technology is not the only thing changing: new television forms – for example, 'reality' television – are transforming the viewing experience, providing new forms of mediated communication. Next we discuss EPGs – how they are shaping viewing practices, reducing engagement as they allow more extended 'grazing', and contributing to profoundly new styles of television viewing. Finally, we report, very briefly, our findings regarding teletext.

Television is more or less important to different people at different times. Television viewing is commonly seen and discussed in polarised ways - as either the end of civilisation or a liberating and pleasurable experience. Watching television is a matter of time use, lifestyle and identity. Television provides sound and moving images that serve as a background to the comings and goings of the household. It is used for relaxation and companionship and as a focus for 'doing nothing'.[44] We found a diversity of expectations regarding television use, from an almost religious commitment to particular soaps or sports programmes to more mundane uses. Many of our research subjects said that television is not that important in their daily lives, they can take it or leave it, and that they have low expectations of the quality of programming – though many watch it for a long time.[45]

A number of members of our households saw their family's television viewing as

---

44   David Gauntlett and Annette Hill (1999) *Television Living. Television, Culture and Everyday Life*, London, Routledge, in association with the British Film Institute; Ann Gray (1992) *Video Playtime: The Gendering of a Leisure Technology*, London, Routledge.

45   As Paddy Scannell states: 'It is hard to give good reasons for watching and listening. We do so because we can't find anything else, anything better to do. In this way, the activities of listeners and viewers appear unmotivated. They are nothing more (or less) than pastimes, ways of spending "free time"'. Paddy Scannell (1996) *Radio, Television and Modern Life: A Phenomenological Approach*, Oxford, Blackwell, p. 24.

passive and negative, and as a waste of time compared with more utilitarian pursuits. News and current affairs were seen by some as more worthy than grazing or more passive viewing.[46] Such moral judgements led to another researcher finding that, except regarding news or current affairs, people felt the need to explain or defend or justify their viewing habits: watching fiction had to be excused, while watching the news was a civic duty.[47] There can be no doubt that entertainment is the major use of television even if governments tend to focus on its use to inform.[48]

We found television commonly used for fairly mundane purposes. When watched alone it seems to hold much lower expectations than when used in group settings, or as a hearth for the household. Commonly, viewing (or not) acts as a background to other activities, or as wallpaper to relieve boredom. This raises questions about the nature and significance of 'television viewing', about how actively a viewer is engaged with a broadcast programme.

> "I don't know really, I just watch whatever's on. I switch off when I watch television to be honest, it's just something to do most of the time, although *EastEnders* is something I enjoy and I like *Pop Idol* as well on a Saturday night, that's started to get really good. You know, it's just that sometimes you like to sit and watch something and not have to think too much about it ... you know, it's not like there's ever anything amazing on, most of the time I watch it for the sake of it. I don't think, 'right there's something I really want to watch so I'll switch it on', it's just there switched on and sometimes a good programme comes on and you kind of perk up a bit ... I suppose I use the TV as a way to relax, it's not the main thing in my life."
> *Nicola Davies, 12 January 2002*

> She told me that she'll watch the television if she's doing the ironing: "sometimes I'll take the ironing in the living room and watch the big TV".
> *Elizabeth Daniels, 27 July 2001*

46   Ingunn Hagen (2000) 'Modern dilemmas: television audiences' time use and moral evaluation' in I. Hagen and J. Wasko *Consuming Audiences?*, Cresskill, NJ, Hampton Press.

47   Pertti Alasuutari found that watching television is associated with laziness and hedonism – one simply sits there passively – and too much viewing is seen as 'wasted time'. He found that the more educated and more middle class were more likely to devalue television viewing, but that everyone in his study valued every activity higher than watching television. He found television to be a moral issue because it is a 'time stealer', and found a hierarchy from news or information to entertainment, with selective viewing morally preferable to grazing or viewing as a couch potato. See P. Alasuutari (1999) 'Introduction: three phases of reception studies' in P. Alasuutari (ed.) *Rethinking the Media Audience. The New Agenda*, London, Sage.

48   James Lull (1990) *Inside Family Viewing: Ethnographic Research on Television Audiences*, London, Routledge.

"By the time I've cooked for us and seen to the horses I'm ready for a drink. I don't really care what's on most of the time."
Elizabeth Daniels, 1 December 2001

When alone she will "put it on for company I suppose".
Ann Thomas, 2 July 2001

In the Swaine household, television provides a babysitting service, vital to parents with demanding children and lifestyles.[49]

She said that it is difficult for her as a working mother to have no help at home during the evenings. She has to cook and clean, while the demands of the children for attention focus solely on her. They tend to 'play up' more often now, because they know that John will be there only at the weekend. The media devices in the home seem to be used by Michelle as a means by which she can focus the attention of the children, enabling her to look after them in a way that is commensurate with her limited time. Michelle and John both work full-time, which has enabled them to buy and pay for the media devices in their home. These allow the children's attention to be positioned away from the parents. Michelle, in particular, would have no time to fulfil her many roles within the family if the children did not have, for example, televisions in their rooms, a VCR or, particularly, Sky television. This is not to suggest that the Swaines have neglected their roles as parents, but rather that the media in their home have allowed them the time to fulfil these roles as well as they can, under the constraints of time and the other pressures of being in full-time work.

"To be honest, there's always something on for the kids and when they watch something, they're glued to it; you couldn't drag them away from it. It's the only time I get to actually do anything around here."
Michelle Swaine, 23 October 2001

"The children learned a lot off *Barney*" (a children's show presented by a large pink dinosaur). She told me that she felt that Nickelodeon and Fox Kids were channels that she felt comfortable leaving the children to watch alone, although she was usually there with them.
Michelle Swaine, 13 July 2001

---

49 Elliott Medrich found that: 'The poor and the less well-educated – those with fewer material and cultural resources and those who often live with less privacy in crowded homes, represent the majority of constant TV households.' E. Medrich (1979) 'Constant television: a background to everyday life', *Journal of Communication*, vol. 26, no. 3, p. 175.

In other households we found that particular programmes were an important part of people's lives.

> The girls watched *Coronation Street* on HTV and then *EastEnders* on BBC1 while we each drank wine. They enjoyed *EastEnders* far more. The social drama unfolding on the screen seemed to stimulate chat about the characters as if they were real people. "He's such a shit, that bloke", Nicola commented about one of the characters, Phil Mitchell. Hannah said, "why doesn't he leave her and the baby alone". They were heavily absorbed in the story line of a tug of love involving the paternity of a young baby girl. The half hour of *EastEnders* seemed quite an intense experience for them, both seemed engaged and focused on the programme throughout and I could sense a release in tension afterwards. It would seem to have cathartic properties. Discussing it later, Nicola said, "I know it's over the top, but I really enjoy it, it's the only thing I *have* to watch. I hate missing it."
> *Nicola Davies, 11 January 2002*

While Nicola sometimes watches television with her daughter, most of the time they are watching it separately. This is facilitated by multiple television sets and VCRs. The VCR is one important way in which viewers can enhance their control and enjoyment of broadcasting. Nicola Davies, who receives only terrestrial, told us about her use of the VCR as an entertainment device for her daughter.

> "The video's more for Lou to watch films, she had *Toy Story* and *The Little Mermaid* for Christmas and it's a good way to keep her entertained, especially if I'm trying to do something ... I don't really use it to record, because I'm mostly here, if there's something I really want to watch. Sometimes I hire a video if someone pops round, but only once a fortnight or something ... I'd like a DVD, because they've got a better picture. My Dad says to wait until they can record from the TV."
> *Nicola Davies, 11 January 2002*

Choice or diversity of television viewing has also been extended by having multiple televisions in households. In most households there is considerable privatised consumption of television within the home – exacerbating the privatisation involved in the home being the major site of leisure and entertainment. This raises concerns about fragmentation and isolation within households; but at the same time privatised media consumption by teenagers in bedrooms can maintain family relations by allowing independence in a context of the safety and security of the family home.[50]

"I've got a television in the living room, a radio in the kitchen with a CD player as well; that's portable, but I mainly listen to it in the kitchen. I've got a portable television in my bedroom as well, if I can't sleep I'll watch it after Louise has gone to bed. It's too quiet downstairs when she goes to bed, so I usually go to bed quite early and watch television until I fall asleep. I've got a remote by the bed, so I just flick it off when I'm ready."
Nicola Davies, 12 January 2002

Seven of our households had digital television, with either a Sky receiver or cable. Some had new DVD technology and cinema sound, and others link their television to hi-fi systems for better sound. In these cases the living room is being filled with improvements to television viewing that increasingly centralise the space for entertainment and information. The living room's role as entertainment centre and public space of the household is reinforced or extended. Geoff Protheroe has spent a considerable amount of money constructing his media 'hearth' – to use the metaphor that has been prevalent in accounts of radio and television.[51]

"I've decided to upgrade to a wide-screen television. I've been looking around on the Internet and I've decided that the Dolby pro logic sets are about the best. I can connect my digital box, video to it and then it gives the programmes and films surround-sound without having to have speakers connected like before ... it's a state of the art 32" flat screen television. I've been meaning to get one for a while and it makes sense to get a good one. I think the flat screen will look better in the living room. My son's just bought one and he thinks it's far better than any other set. My wife thinks it's a complete waste of money, but then she would."
Geoff Protheroe, 26 January 2002

The James' home exemplifies how the living room is becoming more focused as a zone of entertainment.

Near the television was a large stock of videos and audio CDs covering an eclectic mix. The stock of blank tapes have several layers of labels on them, indicating that they have been used many times to record programmes of interest. The stereo, television, PlayStation and Sky receiver occupied this corner space, suggesting that this room functioned as a focal point for

---

50   David Morley (1992) *Television, Audiences and Cultural Studies*, London, Routledge.
51   Simon Frith (1983) 'The pleasures of the hearth' in *Formations of Pleasure*, London, RKP; Paddy Scannell and David Cardiff (1991) *A Social History of British Broadcasting. Volume 1 1922–1939: Serving the Nation*, Oxford, Blackwell.

family 'get together time' and that they were used frequently for this purpose.
James household, 29 August 2001

At the Swaines, too, we saw how digital technology has contributed to the centralisation of media devices in the living room.

> The household has a modestly sized living room – two small rooms that have been knocked into one. By the front window the children have a pool table set up, and in the lounge section there is a large television with Sky Digital (and a VCR), which takes up a considerable amount of room. It is the main focus of the room and is constantly on. The television and in particular Sky, is the staple of the household. It remained on during all my time there, apart from when I spoke to John alone. There is a computer in the living room, but it seems redundant.
> *Swaine household, 23 May 2001*

With cable and satellite, people can listen to music, watch films, play games, shop and communicate via their television sets. Devices that may have been spread around the living room are increasingly designed to be stacked neatly below large, cinema-like, wide-screen television sets. There is more on offer and a larger screen in the living room. This is illustrated by the Powell household.

> The family tends to use the living room and conservatory as the main areas to sit and read the newspaper, or watch television. The living room houses the 28-inch wide-screen television, VCR, DVD player and the Sky digital receiver. So most of the entertainment devices are in this area. There is a large collection of films, including musicals, comedy, action and sports videos. Rhian flicked to the film guide to see what was on for us to watch. The film *The Green Mile* was due to start in five minutes and was being shown on three channels every hour. The three decided that they wanted to watch this. Rhian exclaimed, "I've just got time to make a drink before it starts, switch over to it, Gareth". Brian switched the volume up. His television was hooked up to the hi-fi speakers and the sound became more focused.
> *Powell household, 1 November 2001*

Other devices no longer compete with the television for use. Instead, they have become intertwined and are designed to operate in conjunction with one another for optimal performance. The upshot is that television is becoming multi-functional, operating with connected devices that together centralise leisure. Activities and pleasures of use become more closely tied to the location of the main television set in the household. Thus the living room is becoming a more public space in households.

> Paul's friends, Darren and Richard, arrived together soon after. They had just finished work and had met up to come around to Paul's as arranged. They told me that they usually meet on a Thursday night to have a social gathering in each other's houses in turn. The structure of these gatherings usually involved watching DVDs or videos, playing console or PC games, and a short visit to the local pub for last orders. Tonight the lads were in Paul's flat. Paul connected the DVD and television to his hi-fi to maximise the sound performance. Darren told me that he had set the trend by spending £700 on a Technics home cinema system that enabled him to have cinema sound at home. Both the friends had brought some alcohol with them; the film *Blade* (a gory vampire movie, based on a comic book character) was to be a backdrop to the social event, with the loud and high quality of the sound requiring or sustaining a very focused form of viewing. *Addey and Rowlands household, 28 June 2001*

Gareth Powell provides a good example of individuals coming out of the bedroom to use the new hearth.

> "I'll go downstairs to watch something on Sky because I can't get it upstairs. Sometimes we'll watch Sky Movies together. Or if they're out, I can flick through the channels. It's not so bad with Dad, 'cos he'll watch most things, but Mam hates me flicking and thinks most of the stuff I watch is rubbish." *Gareth Powell, 1 November 2001*

In multi-channel households, not only did we find a reduction in the use of older media devices, but also the loss of the traditional associations of this older equipment. Playing music on a hi-fi or watching a film from a VCR are being replaced by games machines with DVD players which do everything. In the process, the cognitive associations of particular devices are being lost – for example, the association of hi-fi with audio quality: many no longer believe that a good hi-fi is better than a simulated one on a PC soundcard. The breadth of devices that normally demonstrate taste, wealth or expertise are being replaced by one single device, digital television – which provides Internet access, games-playing, cinema sound and digital radio. The multi-functionality and ease of use of this device reduces the need to own VCRs, hi-fis, games consoles and PCs, and in the process changes the forms of distinction with which these devices are associated. In some of our households the trend is thus a reduction in the number of devices that are being used, and in some the radio, hi-fi and VCR look likely to become obsolete.

In households with multi-channel television we found reduced use of the VCR.

> Paul has cable digital television and a PlayStation 2 (PS2) which is used as a games console, DVD player, CD audio player and connects to the Internet, all for less then £300. "I hardly use the stereo anymore, or the video."
> *Paul Addey, 16 October 2001*

In much the same way the James family reported that they never go to the video shop anymore. They used to go a lot at the weekend to hire a film, but now have Sky Box Office which allows access to all the latest movies at £2.50 a time.

> They have a greater choice of the newer movies, they told me, "without the hassle of having to drive into town to hire one for the night and then return it".
> *James household, 29 August 2001*

On the other hand, 24-hour programming and greater choice provided the impetus to use the VCR. Both of the Daniels boys record sports events from Sky because they are shown from around the world and so are often broadcast when they are out for the night, or early in the morning. The Lewis household, having given up Sky, use the VCR more.

The boys were in the centre living room out of the way of the others. I entered the room to find Rhodri on the armchair and Dafydd on the small sofa, both glued to *The Simpsons* on BBC2. The room was full of videos, mostly comedy and sport, with the occasional Disney film for Hannah. The boys showed me the *Rocky* box set, which they had recently bought at HMV in Swansea. Among their video collection were the *Aliens Trilogy*, the BBC Wales comedy *Grand Slam*, the American series *Friends* and several rugby and soccer videos. Rhodri set the VCR to record *EastEnders*; and said that they also record films they miss if they are out for the night. The boys really wanted to re-subscribe to Sky. Since they had stopped having Sky they have had to go to the video shop twice a week to hire films. Karen is reluctant to re-subscribe because of the cost; this seems to be a bone of contention between her and the boys at the moment. The use of television by the boys is therefore a mix of terrestrial channels, hired videos and

PlayStation games.
Lewis household, 20 September 2001

Boundaries between information and entertainment are becoming blurred with
new technology but also with the development of more hybridised programme
formats. 'Reality' television programmes and extended news coverage have
eroded the boundaries between fact and fiction.[52] News has become entertainment, while entertainment has taken a more realist and harsh edge (for example,
Weakest Link, Big Brother). In the context of broadcasting, distinctions between
fiction and real life are becoming more difficult, if not impossible, to sustain.[53]

> I arrived later that night to find the lads both watching live coverage of *Big
> Brother* on E4 (Channel 4 digital). They sat and watched the night's events
> unfold at the house with the knowledgeability of avid soap fans, tuned in
> to the drama and subplots of the interaction and dynamics of the *Big
> Brother* house. They described it as voyeuristic and said that my research
> at their home was not different from the programme, in that it is 'fly on
> the wall'. It looks at the same kinds of issues as they found entertaining in
> this style of 'reality' television. I attempted to distinguish between sociology
> and psychology, but felt that they found the comparison between them-
> selves and the *Big Brother* participants rather pleasing. It was interesting
> that their comments on the artificial environment of the *Big Brother* house
> seemed to suggest that my time with them was also in some sense artificial.
> I agreed with them on this point. This represented an interesting and honest
> exchange between researcher and participants regarding the impact of my
> presence on their activities and behaviour.
> *Addey and Rowlands household, 26 June 2001*

The status given to the programme and the level of attention and engagement
of the viewer with a programme are important for how television is used as
background, information or entertainment. In many respects, the level of focus
depends on the distance the viewer places themselves from the subjects they are
viewing on the screen. 'Reality' television challenges this cognitive distance on
the part of the viewer. Television is becoming more voyeuristic, replicating the

---

52 Richard Kilborn (1994) 'How real can you get? recent developments in 'reality' television', *European
Journal of Communication*, vol. 9, no. 4, pp. 421–439.

53 Neil Postman argues that the processing of reality by producers and viewers blurs the distinction between
reality and fantasy. He takes this further, arguing that, with no context or sequence, television is incapable
of rational argument. While it may be fine for fantasy and pleasure, he sees television as dangerous for
understanding reality. See N. Postman (1986) *Amusing Ourselves to Death: Public Discourse in the Age of
Showbusiness*, London, Methuen.

feel of the Internet, and bringing the audience closer with the content, with those on the screen. It does this, however, while maintaining the safety of distance for viewers: what is on screen seems in some sense reality, but it is on the screen, so viewers feel comfortable with it, or distanced from it. Thus these new television forms seem to be viewed in a more involved process.

> Following the programme on mob violence and a violent and dangerous game show, Ann indicated that she had had enough of Sky One for the evening and turned to *Big Brother* on Channel 4. She said that with digital, "sometimes I don't really know what channel we're watching". Stuart seemed to be quite entertained by the programmes. "If producers can get away with making it, people will watch it, it's human nature." He said that the documentary style gives the programmes a guise of being educational, and that the shows were too intense to simply be background viewing. He comments that people "are glued to it, eventually madness on the screen will become the norm". Ann's initial comment was that "I hope Britain never goes down this line of TV programming ... I would be disgusted if the BBC did this, they do 999, but it's far more tasteful". She comments that the level of violence on Sky was not acceptable. "You get this stuff on the Internet, but that's a personal choice. You don't want it in your face, though you find it on the net, with TV it's more in your face."
> *Ann Thomas, 3 July 2001*

Violence on Sky was another issue of contention in the Chandler and Thomas household.

> *Fear Factor* is a show in which people have to undertake dangerous stunts to win a $50,000 prize. The first stunt to be attempted was to run as far as possible while being pursued by a police dog. Contestants wore protective suits, and the dogs savagely held them to the ground by their arms while contestants struggled to increase their distance. Although padded, it seemed as if the contestants were in some pain, and all showed a degree of fear. Other challenges consisted of lying in a pit of snakes for two minutes, walking along a beam suspended a hundred foot in the air, and being covered in insects. The show's motto was 'To stare fear in the eye'. Stuart seemed to find it entertaining, laughing loudly as the contestants struggled with the police dogs.

> Ann came downstairs as Sky One was showing a programme about mobs and rioting world-wide. They both sat transfixed as the quasi-documen-

tary showed graphic footage of civil unrest from across the world. The programme was sensationalist, with occasional soundbites on the psychology of violence and human nature.

Stuart and Ann reacted to this programme in different ways, with Ann less at ease with the violent scenes than Stuart. Ann said that she would like to watch something else: "What is this show, it's bizarre", Stuart said, "They must be pushing the boundaries a bit here." Ann sat uncomfortably in her seat, while Stuart leaned forward. "Stuart likes this kind of thing", she said.
Chandler and Thomas household, 3 July 2001

While Stuart's taste in music, science fiction, history and fantasy seemed better catered for by digital channels, Ann prefers terrestrial television – though they both enjoy *The Blue Planet*, *Friends* and *Frasier*. She regards terrestrial television as the foundation of her viewing, with Sky programmes a supplement. "If there's nothing on the normal channels then I'll flick around on Sky."

Sports programming was another issue of conflict in some multi-channel households.

Rhian Powell left the room to have a bath after watching *Invasion* with Brian – a programme about the architecture of war in Britain, on the Discovery channel. Gareth came down soon after and he and Brian watched Australian Rules football – explaining the rules as it went along.

"Sky Sport cover all kinds of sport from around the world, sometimes you'll be watching ice hockey or baseball, then Sumo or something, it's really good if you're a sports addict", said Brian. Rhian returned some time later and told Brian, in no uncertain terms, to switch over from the sport. They all decided they would watch a film on Sky Movies that they had not seen before.

Rhian likes the Discovery channel, "but they're not a patch on BBC documentaries and wildlife programmes. *The Blue Planet* is the best they've ever done", Brian responded, "it's nearly good enough to warrant charging us the licence fee … I'm not too particular what I watch as long as it's entertaining. There's not much on the four normal channels that I'll watch apart from the news."
Powell household, 1 November 2001

As well as new programme formats, we explored new ways in which programmes are selected and accessed. We found that EPGs, on-screen menus and weekly planners in multi-channel households have changed how households gather information to plan their media use and the process of watching television, the mode of viewing. Only three of our households use only printed television listings to plan their viewing for the evening. Multi-channel households use EPGs, but still mix and match their programme information sources.

We explored whether our households used digital services and EPGs to plan their consumption of the media. Digital television provides an on-screen programme listing for the week ahead. This can be navigated using the remote control, which is the tool by which the whole digital interactive package is accessed. Use of these services varied between households. With about 60 channels in most of our digital households, the EPG is shaping how programmes and channels are selected in some households – with on-screen menus an integral part of progressing through the multitude of channels, options and interactive features. The EPG is fast becoming the first point of call when the television is switched on in our NTL and Sky households. So the concerns of broadcasters in Wales and elsewhere about the positioning of their channel on the EPG are very real. S4C, though on 104 on Sky in Wales, appears on 752 on NTL (in Wales as in the rest of the UK); and in 2003 viewers were warned that BBC1 Wales was to move from 101 to 942 and BBC2 Wales from 102 to 961 on Sky in Wales, though this never happened. The broadcasters' concern is the negative effect for casual viewers; the children's menu on the EPG, for example, does not include any Welsh programmes (because it lists only *channels*, not *programmes* – so ignores S4C's *Planed Plant*).

EPGs are used in various ways, which connect with issues of time and routine. In a sense they allow greater control when watching television. Individuals can work out what they want to watch and when, and then act accordingly, without the need to use a paper publication for television listings.

> Christopher Rowlands said that he used to buy the *TV Times* but now relies on the listings on NTL to give a full breakdown of the night's entertainment ahead. His night is very much focused on the choice and range of programmes and media devices at his disposal. He uses the DVD and the VCR in conjunction with pre-planned choices of programmes, using the EPG to plan what to record on the VCR. Alternatively, he may watch a DVD, if there is nothing worth watching at that time.
> *Addey and Rowlands household, 17 June 2001*

It appears that EPGs are used in a more synchronic way than paper listings, that is, that they are used as an instant resource, to inform about what is on at the present time.

> *"Y peth gorau yw does dim rhaid chwilio trwy'r papurau newydd i weld beth sy' ar, neu eistedd trwy hanner awr o rhyw rhaglen er mwyn darganfod beth mae o amdan."* ["The great thing is that you don't have to search through the papers to find out what's on, or sit through half an hour of a programme to find out what it's about."]
> *Gwyn James, 29 August 2001*

> We sat and talked until around nine at night, when Mark left to meet Iona, his girlfriend. Gwyn switched the television on and searched for a film for the rest of us to watch. There was no dispute over the programming and Gwyn used the EPG to inform Ieuan what the film was about. We watched *The Crossing*, a film about the American War of Independence on Sky Movies.
> *James household, 29 August 2001*

The Daniels boys use the EPG to plan their video recording when they are out. This is quicker than using the newspaper listings which, they say, do not list the more obscure channels anyway.

We found that individuals like to get their programme information from a number of sources, instead of relying exclusively on electronic programme planners. The most popular of these, and all that is available in terrestrial households, is the television listings in newspapers and magazines. Local newspapers were commonly reported to be bought mainly for the television listings and reviews. Again, we can distinguish between planning what to watch and looking to see what is on.

> I noticed that *The Evening Post* had remained in the kitchen. Mrs Daniels told me, "the boys tend to flick through that to see what's on television or at the cinema when they're home".
> *Elizabeth Daniels, 21 July 2001*

> From the living room I could hear the television on upstairs, where Ann was spending time alone watching television. Stuart was watching Sky One, and he showed me that the menu and programme guide allows you to have a full listing for up to seven days ahead. Ann buys a television guide for the programme listings for the television upstairs, which is not connected to Sky. She buys it "because it's easier than coming downstairs to find out what's on". Later Ann told me that she buys either *TV Weekly* or

TV Quick for her weekly listings of programmes on terrestrial and satellite. Stuart went on to show me a facility on Sky that provides a summary of the programme or episode as you choose the channel. This facility allows you to see a brief description of the content of the episode or show before you view. Stuart was showing me this during the opening credits of *The Simpsons*, which he was going to watch on Sky One.
Chandler and Thomas household, 3 July 2001

Generally, EPGs seem to be used as a quick reference resource rather than a longer term planning resource, and we found that the more advanced EPG facilities were not used. Sky and NTL have a personal programme planner, and a flagging system – which none of our households use.

"Yeah, you can flag programmes you want to be reminded of, you can even have a programme planner for the week ahead, the television reminds you that there's a programme on you want to watch. I don't do that, but you can if you want."
Paul Addey, 15 September 2001

EPGs are complex, and in a state of flux as programmes start and finish. For some, they confuse as much as they inform. The extent to which digital interactive services and EPGs are used varies, with a gender dimension to this patterning (discussed in Chapter 4). In many of our households, the digital services and EPG are seen as too complex to navigate.

"I'll have some sherry and sit and watch television with the dog. I don't know what I watch really, I'll just see what's on. I don't bother with Sky unless someone else is watching it. I can't work the thing, it's too complicated." Mrs Daniels and I sat in the living room, the television was on showing the BBC News 24, and Mrs Daniels flicked through the channels and ended up with UK Gold showing a repeat of *Open All Hours* with Ronnie Barker. "I tend to watch whatever's on at the time."
Elizabeth Daniels, 12 September 2001

Much of the time was spent watching Geoff trying to get Sky to work, while Angharad and I talked. Occasionally she spoke to Geoff, but he ignored her, as he was fully engrossed in his battle with the remote control. Geoff could not operate the system to switch from terrestrial to Sky. "I hardly use the thing, I can't remember how I did it the last time." Both he and Angharad struggled to operate the system, seemingly unsure if it was a technical fault or their lack of know-how. It took some time for them to finally get Sky

News, much to their delight. It struck me that this was not a household where they watched a lot of digital television.
Protheroe household, 14 September 2001

The complexity of EPG listings, paradoxically, makes paper listings relatively attractive.

"Michelle gets *TV Quick*, we just look at that, I don't bother looking at the guides, it's too confusing. I only watch it before my shift starts and on the weekends."
John Swaine, 12 July 2001

Paper guides offer more than the listings. Nicola Davies knows what she wants to watch, and when these programmes are broadcast, but she buys *TV Quick* for the stories about programmes – which are not provided via the EPG.

"It's only something like 20p. I read it in work during a break. It's not just a television guide, it's got behind-the-scenes reports and tells you what's coming up in the soaps and stuff like that ... It's an all-right read and I keep it for the TV guide for the week."
Nicola Davies, 29 November 2001

While some still plan their viewing, multi-channel households tend to flick through the channels. While EPGs would seem logically to eradicate the need to do this, it is clear that this mode of viewing takes place in almost all multi-channel households. Flicking through the channels has almost become a way of watching television. People flick through the channels from the first to the last, stopping at each programme for a couple of seconds, searching for something to watch. These individuals use an EPG but flick as a way of selecting a programme, or even as a mode of viewing.

Brian flicked through the channels to see what was on Sky. He did not use the EPG, he just went through one by one. He went around the channels before finally returning to Sky Sports. By this time they had changed the coverage to show boxing. Brian settled with this and poured himself a whisky from his sideboard drinks cabinet. "I like to have a drink before bed. Rhian soaks in the bath after her day, I'll have a whisky and I'm set for the night ... We don't bother with the TV guides, I'll flick through the list of channels to look for something specific, but I don't spend ages there planning my night like some people, I suppose?"
Brian Powell, 1 November 2001

Navigating with cable and satellite is more like using the Web. Like that, it often means being led up the garden path – spending ages looking perhaps in vain for something of use or interest.

The menus can be displayed permanently on the screen, in a window that occupies a part of the screen. The programme being viewed is reduced in size to allow the viewer to keep one eye on the other choices – like multiple windows on a PC. In one of our households in particular, the EPG used in this way is a semi-permanent feature of watching television and has profoundly affected how television is used by encouraging flicking as a mode of viewing. Viewing takes place in shorter bursts, in a less settled mode, with a prominent visual prompt that there is something else, possibly better, coming on on another channel – with the viewer constantly being lured away from what they are watching by the potential alternatives. While over the years various critics have modified Raymond Williams' work on the 'flow' of broadcasting,[54] which was disrupted profoundly by the arrival of the VCR, 'flow' is even more seriously challenged with the advent of multi-channel television. We found in one household an extreme disregard of narrative – which has been seen as the core feature of most programming and research on audiences. A corollary is that the very notion of an audience for a programme becomes even more untenable or meaningless. The Addey and Rowlands household illustrates what seems a profoundly new way of using the television.

He then placed the menu function on and while we watched a programme about snowboarding on E4, all the other options were displayed on screen (at the same time). The remote control stayed nearby, in case a change was wanted. The audio was turned off, allowing purely visual stimulation. The act of eating in front of the television seemed to be appropriate for viewing rather than listening … .

> The television was showing Fox Kids, a cartoon network on cable digital. The interactive guide was also activated, so the screen was bordered on two sides by other programme listings and further menus. This seemed to suggest that the channels might be changed frequently and that a full screen might not be used for a programme, which would only be on as background. The on-screen menu acted as a semi-permanent facilitator of a

54   At the heart of Williams' account is the notion that the television experience is about more than discrete programmes. John Ellis developed this thinking with the notions of 'segmentation' and repetition' as the main features of television output. See Raymond Williams (1974) *Television. Technology and Cultural Form*, London, Fontana; and John Ellis (1982) *Visible Fictions: Cinema, Television, Video*, London, Routledge and Kegan Paul.

quick change to another channel, should his choice of programme not hold his attention.

"I have the menus down so that I know what's going on, before that we used to flick through the channels too much. I still flick through a lot on the way to the channel I want. Sometimes there's just too much going on and it disturbs your enjoyment. If there's something I really want to watch, I'll turn the menu guide off for a while … We plan what we're going to watch as we're doing now, we just flick through the on-screen guide to see what's on. Normally I'll have the guide on all the time, so that the picture is in the centre of the screen and info about the other channels is there as well. If there's something good on, like a film, I'll switch the guide off."
Paul Addey, 26 October 2001

Even our more technologically able households do not use all the interactive features, because they are unreliable. Christopher Rowlands found this consistently with his Internet, telephone and television package provider.

"Hang on [turns to interactive page], there you have it [quotes from the screen] *'this service is currently not available'*. It's always offline, it never works, so we don't bother. Bloody NTL, they're shit!"
Christopher Rowlands, 29 June 2001

Paul has an email address and Internet access through NTL television, but experiences difficulty in logging on sometimes and has difficulty receiving emails as well. "The problem is, that you have to pay extra for the keyboard from NTL, I use the control, but it takes ages to write an email, it's just too long. I only use it to email mates, so I can text them on my mobile anyway, it's just a gimmick at the moment … I have used it to surf, but it's not as good as a PC, you can't get all the flash graphics, just text and stills."
Paul Addey, 29 June 2001.

The use of digital interactive can be quite a complicated business.

Tennis coverage from Wimbledon was on the television as I arrived; Stuart told me that he was watching BBC1. He then showed me the interactive feature that the BBC has introduced this year. He switched to Sky Digital and selected BBC1 on the channel menu. This brought up coverage of the main match being shown on the terrestrial version, but with an added menu that allows viewers to choose any match from the dozen or so being covered at Wimbledon simultaneously. The interactive option also allows you to watch one match with another minimised in the corner. It provides a

continuous update of all results and scores from all the other games going on, while also giving a full results round-up from all the matches played. In many respects BBC1 received through Sky allows you to browse the whole competition while also being in control of the coverage. Ann was excited about this feature. Stuart, on the other hand, said, "I haven't got much of a clue … I don't really know what's going on". The new interactive coverage seemed to please Ann, who said that she could keep up with the whole day's play and not miss a thing.
Chandler and Thomas household, 7 July 2001

Interactive features mean that the user has to multi-task and to switch between screens, events and commentary, with windows a semi-permanent or background feature of television viewing. Viewers have programmes, menus and interactive features on simultaneously as background or for information, and turn them off during entertainment usage. They have to multi-task to enjoy fully the capabilities and features of digital television. Thus the activity of consuming television has become more user-driven, requiring greater proactivity on the part of the viewer. While electronic guides and interactive features have made the process of viewing too complex for some, for others they have become a normal background to viewing.

What emerged quite clearly is that flicking is becoming an increasingly significant form of viewing in some digital households. With terrestrial there are fewer channels, so flicking between them means a quick return to the start, and the need to settle on one of the (say five) channels available (or watch nothing). With multi-channel television, however, the large number of channels means that some programmes will have changed by the time one returns to them, so continuous channel flicking can constitute a varied, and seemingly acceptable, form of viewing. EPGs perhaps encourage this more promiscuous form of viewing by displaying an Aladdin's cave of choice. The array of channels and information becomes a total sensory experience for the viewer. The ability to navigate such a digital experience is another question. Paul Addey sums up the complex nature of contemporary television use.

"Watching TV these days is a bit like sitting at the flight deck of the starship *Enterprise*; you feel in control but there's a lot going on."
Paul Addey, 17 June 2001

In our research, we found only a few households using teletext.

John was planning a night out for the following weekend, to catch some

live music. He was trying to get a listing of local events through teletext on BBC1. He was having no luck getting any specific local entertainment news and tried Spectel for specifically Welsh information. "I've used it before, I just can't seem to find it now ... I'll probably go and buy the *NME* or *Melody Maker*, maybe they'll have it listed in there ... you'd think Sky would have an information channel wouldn't you?"
John Daniels, 23 September 2001

"I use it to look for sports results at the weekend or in the week. I follow the football and rugby, and it's quicker than reading the papers. It's the same for the television guides, it's easier than buying a paper. I've heard you can find out about cheap holidays on it as well. I'm thinking of going to Spain with the boys next summer, so I'm going to use it to have a look at flights."
Dafydd Lewis, 14 December 2001

The Swaines and Daniels reported that they had used teletext to check on lottery results from time to time, and Mr Daniels said that sometimes he used it for weather reports. Paul Addey and Christopher Rowlands sometimes turned to teletext to find national and regional sports results, and used the 888 function on some Welsh-language programmes to help with learning the language (discussed in Chpter 4). Karen Lewis and her boys used it for the television listings. Generally, however, teletext seems to be the unknown or forgotten medium, perhaps eclipsed by 24-hour news and its interactive facility that allows users to watch weather, sport and news on recorded loops that are updated periodically. Mark James explained to us how teletext has become redundant in their household:

"I used to use text for sports results and news, but now I just press the red interactive button on BBC News 24 and you get all the headlines and sports and lots of other listings at a touch of the button. You don't have to wait for the pages to change like on teletext; it's much quicker and easier and less frustrating. If you want to look for cheap holidays you can just go to the Internet."
Mark James, 7 January 2002

In conclusion, we found much television viewing to be mundane and unimportant. We found varieties of viewing styles, with profound gender variations. We found VCRs and multiple television sets being used to enhance temporal and spatial choice. In digital households, however, we found the living room becoming more of a focal point. The increase in multi-task technologies means that one device performs the tasks of three or four older technologies. This affects the uses and meanings of older media, notably the VCR and (as we discussed in Chapter 3) radio. In displacing these, the television has been elevated to become a more central medium in the home. The television in multi-channel households has become like the hearth again, the focus for coming together in the living room.

People are still watching television together and in technological terms it is increasingly sophisticated. 'Reality' television and digital interactive have blurred traditional distinctions between broadcasters and the audience. New modes of viewing have emerged, such as flicking, using interactive features and using EPGs in windows-like ways. Watching television has become more complex. For some this means that it has become unusable, since some the features of digital and EPGs are too complex to grasp. They have reverted to print for television listings. For others, the user-based interface provides greater autonomy, choice and control.

New media

Older media are far from static, transforming constantly as society, culture and technology develop.[55] In recent years, however, we have seen the emergence of new media that seem, at least potentially, to challenge the older media. Their greatest significance may lie in the impact they are having on older media – which are developing new forms, using new technologies and being regulated in new ways. Nonetheless, new media are also important in their own right, in that they are winning time and space in households. Like other media, they serve both to bring people together and to construct personal space. We found three new media of particular significance: computer games, the Internet and email.

Computer games

First we examine how games consoles are used as a form of entertainment, one that often results in fragmentation in households and conflict over space. We examine the location and use of games consoles and discuss how gaming is a highly social activity, one that brings people together. We explore how games consoles are becoming accepted as an important form of entertainment in the home and how they have come to occupy the space and achieve the standing that they enjoy. We shall explore how gaming involves the construction of imagined but very real communities.

---

55   Brian Winston (1986) *Understanding Media*, London, Routledge & Kegan Paul.

Of the six households with games consoles, only two had their console in a bedroom and these were households with only one games player. The others had the machine connected to the television set, in the living room. This location of games-playing devices suggests that gaming is a social or group activity.

Gamers are keen to keep up with the latest technologies: one of our households acquired two state of the art systems (Sega Dreamcast and PlayStation 2) during the course of our research.

> Since my last visit, Paul had bought a new games console, a PlayStation 2. The PS2 had cost Paul £299 and had taken ages to arrive after it had been ordered. At around £40 a game, ownership of the console is not a cheap affair.
>
> "It cost a fortune and the games are really expensive, but it's a great machine, it's a DVD player as well and it plays all my audio CDs. It's good because it plays all the old PlayStation games, so I can still play them as well. The best thing about it is that you can play online with this machine and surf the Web ... It's a bit expensive and you can only play against other PS2 users because the format of the games on a PC is different."
>
> Although the machine is expensive, Paul sees it as value for money. "Well it's a DVD player as well isn't it, so I'm getting into buying DVD films as well."
> *Paul Addey, 27 September 2001*

For some, gaming is a solitary, highly individualistic, activity that can dominate an individual's time. Single player games are often based on strategy, or are plot-driven. They are not as entertaining to watch as to play, and in their nature are long, complex and engaging.

> Stuart came downstairs and we sat and chatted about his video collection and large collection of PlayStation games. Stuart is certainly not an occasional games player. He said that his games-playing in the living room does not cause any domestic conflict; Ann's laughter could be heard from the kitchen, indicating that Stuart's comments were contentious. He has a large collection of single-player PlayStation games (*Command and Conquer, Civilization, Worms, Sim City*). He prefers strategy-based games, which take a long time to complete.
> *Stuart Chandler, 21 June 2001*

Thus Stuart occupies the living space with his own entertainment. When he does so Ann retreats to the television upstairs; and they told us that their arguments about this have led to him playing games less.

Gaming can involve a decline in the uses of other media or of other activities.

> "I don't tend to watch as much television now, I still watch a fair bit, but I'll play *Red Faction* if I'm here on my own, or *Quake3* if Rowlands is here. Otherwise I'm in work, or in the pub."
> *Paul Addey, 27 September 2001*

> "Well, I've been in a lot lately since my bird dumped me, I haven't got much else to do, perhaps I'm a bit sad, I don't know ... perhaps I bought it because I don't go out as much."
> *Paul Addey, 15 October 2001*

In some households, on the other hand, there has been a decline in the use of games consoles, with former enthusiasts hardly playing at all as other media have taken over and lifestyles have changed. Stuart Chandler said that his game-playing had decreased since they had subscribed to Sky. Several of our respondents reported that they had moved away from a high level of gaming.

> "I'm never here these days, anyway, I've gone off computer games at the moment, real life's a whole lot better!"
> *Christopher Rowlands, 17 June 2001*

Another distinguished himself from his younger brother in this respect, identifying himself as more mature.

> "We do swap with people from school, but not as much as I used do. There's magazines for the PlayStation but we don't get them anymore. Sometimes you have reviews in magazines like *Loaded* and *FHM*, that's the sort of things I buy now. Rhodri is more into that, but I've sort of grown out of it. I still play, but we don't get together to play as much anymore."
> *Dafydd Lewis, 14 December 2001*

To be a good gamer takes time and practice, which can generate conflict over space. The location of consoles – in the living room in all but two of our game-playing households – leads to conflict over when and what types of games are played. Karen Lewis explains that her younger son Rhodri is the main games player in the house.

> "He plays for hours, but less now because his social life has improved. Dafydd is definitely TV first then PlayStation, whereas Rhodri is PlaySta-

tion then TV. They play against one another, I remember I bought it a few Christmases ago, the sounds of Christmas joy were replaced by a whole lot of swearing because Rhodri was beating Dafydd all the time. This sends Dafydd crazy, because Rhodri is much better at the games. He's [Rhodri] got more patience and is more logical. Dafydd'll pick it up and play for a short time, while Rhodri'll see the game as a challenge and want to get to the end ... They will play together for a while, but there's some friction over who wants to watch television or play PlayStation, but Dafydd usually gives in."
Karen Lewis, 14 December 2001

We asked Dafydd whether he and Rhodri used the PlayStation together or alone.

"It depends really, if we're here at the same time we play against each other, Rhodri prefers games like *Command and Conquer* and I prefer sports sims like *Nba Jam* and *Jonah Lomu Rygbi* ... if there's something I want to watch on, I'll watch it, Rhodri can play it when I'm out, but when I'm home I'm in charge."
Dafydd Lewis, 14 December 2001

In households with a Gameboy or other console in the bedroom, conflict over space is less of an issue. Gareth Powell's gaming takes place in his bedroom – using single-player, plot-driven games – but he rarely plays. Christopher Swaine has a Gameboy and is transfixed by it whenever and wherever he plays. He can play anywhere in the house so his gaming does not interfere with the activities of others, but it tends to shut him out of the goings-on around him. A hand-held games machine – resembling some uses of the newspaper – can be used as a means of cutting oneself off from one's surroundings.

Christopher was quietly playing *Super Mario Land* on his Gameboy. Michelle told me that he loved the thing, that he was always playing it. She showed concern that the small screen might be bad for his eyes or give him headaches. Christopher was transfixed by the screen, oblivious to Michelle's voice asking him what he had had for dinner at school. Eventually we found out that he had had burger and chips, after many attempts and a little translation of the mumbled response. It was hard to tell if Christopher was using the Gameboy as a means to ignore Michelle's queries about homework; he would occasionally look up to watch the television. Christopher was happy to be in the company of his parents; his time alone

was spent in the world created by the Gameboy.
Swaine household, 13 July 2001

Gaming, however, is not generally such an individual activity. More commonly it is very much a collective, albeit highly competitive, activity. In households with two or more game players, multi-player gaming seems to be the most popular mode of playing – with racing and combat games the most popular. In the Addey and Rowlands household the social aspect of gaming has been taken to an extreme as a collective ritual. Household members play individually and against each other, but they have taken multi-playing to a gladiatorial level, with their social life revolving around gaming.

> Paul has bought a few games for the console: *Grand Tourismo 3* (a racing simulator) *Red Faction* (a tactical shoot 'em up) and *Quake Arena* (a multi-player shoot 'em up). His favourite is *Quake*, because it is a multi-player game. Up to four players can play at once, more if playing online, or if two or more machines are connected using a special port and cable. Paul told me that he and his friend, who also owns a PS2, get together and about eight of them play at once.

> "We usually play here before we go to the pub, or over my mate's, it depends on what night it is. We usually get together once a week and the scores are saved on the machine."

> The lads record their status and performance and there is an ongoing ranking competition between the friends. Paul's friends are all keen games players and the games are very competitive, hence his practice – to enhance his credibility.
> *Paul Addey, 27 September 2001*

The PS2 was a focus for group interaction and competition on a weekly basis in the Addey and Rowlands household. It seemed that participants looked forward to their encounters, rather like members of a football team look forward to Saturday afternoon. The artificial reality of the game produces a very real sense of competition and bravado among the participants. A highly social activity, it transcends the boundaries of the living room or bedroom, becoming an important aspect of the players' social lives, whether in school or the local pub. Gaming is a key element of their identity and binds them together in some sort of community of games players.

> The group consumed a considerable amount of alcohol in a short time and were determined to continue back at Paul's, with a bottle of vodka and a

few rounds of multi-player *Quake*. Two friends, Darren and Richard, returned to the flat. They took up position on the sofa in front of the television, Paul sat cross-legged on the floor and I sat somewhat out of the way to the side. I settled down to watch what had been billed at the pub as the greatest battle on earth. The players chose a character and loaded up the stats, which are kept on the memory card of the console. Each tournament is recorded on this card. The game screen is split diagonally in half with one player on the top and the other in the bottom half. It struck me that the game was very fast. It was difficult to navigate, or even to see where the opposition might be hiding. The lads, however, seemed very skilled and the games were both highly competitive and close-run affairs. The stats were updated all the time, with lower or higher averages than before being praised or ridiculed by the other players. I was invited to play, and my name was included in the league table for that night. My stats were appalling, much to the pleasure of the other players, although I must say that no mercy was shown. It seemed that it was a sink or swim affair. This was serious gaming in action. Winners stayed on, while challengers and champions rotated play. Paul appeared to be one of the more skilled players, while also being the worst loser. The bravado and engagement with the game were very interesting. Playing meant more to the players than simply an evening's entertainment. Tonight's performance would be the talk of the next session in the pub, or would be the cause of grudges or re-plays in the future. The gaming lasted as long as the alcohol, although the drinking was secondary to the contest being played out. I left the house at 2.30 a.m., too tired to stay awake, but the lads were still playing.
Addey and Rowlands household, 16 October 2001

Even in individual play, gamers are bound together by their taste in games, skill levels, hints and tips magazines and reliance on one another for swapping new games (to save money). Thus individualised play, too, involves belonging to some imagined but very real community of gamers.[56]

Karen told me that they got into PlayStation through friends at school and the advertising campaign that Sony aimed at teenagers at the launch of the system. The boys have had the system for three years, having previously

---

56 Resembling in some ways television fandom, in that it is a way of engaging with, rather than withdrawing from, the social world. See Cheryl Harris and Alison Alexander (eds) (1998) *Theorizing Fandom*, New Jersey, Hampton Press.

owned a Nintendo machine.
Karen Lewis, 25 November 2001

This notion of a community of gamers might be most applicable to online gaming. Cost is the main deterrent to playing online, although some reported to us that they had played in the past. Games consoles, however, seem easier to use, and players seem to prefer a real-life opponent who is co-present in the same physical space. Even though individual players have access to the online global community of players, the preferred mode of play in our households was face-to-face.

> Paul has played games online, but prefers to play against friends, " ... besides which, it's really expensive to play online, you forget how long you're on for and it costs a fortune in the end".
> *Paul Addey, 16 October 2001*

> "No it's too expensive on the Dreamcast, I do like online gaming, but not from the flat, down my Mum's, that's the best! Most games I play these days are multi-player racing games or, you know, the fighting games, something where there's a real person to play against."
> *Christopher Rowlands, 16 October 2001*

The low take-up of Internet gaming suggests that participating in virtual communities from home holds less attraction than playing with friends or alone – perhaps because PC games are strategy or role play. The multi-player mode of play seems to facilitate a good night in with friends. There seems a clear disjuncture between how gamers are regarded as solitary and how they see themselves and experience gaming as a social activity.

The Internet

Four of our households had a PC with Internet access and used it. One had access via NTL, but found this unusable. Two had PCs in cupboards and did not use them at all (one of these had Internet access) and three households had no PC or Internet access at all. Perhaps surprisingly, we found that the PC has made few inroads into the home but, rather, is seen and used as a tool – for work, research (finding out about things), shopping and keeping in contact (by email). It is used primarily for work, largely breaking down the boundary between home and work or, in some cases, between home and school. It is used in private by individuals to perform quite specific work or information-seeking tasks. Most usage is pragmatic and time spent on the Internet is relatively short. We found a general feeling that Internet shopping is slightly risky. There seems to be some mistrust of the technology, perhaps because of its associations with the sphere of work. We found little to suggest that the PC is used as a home entertainment device. Rather, it was a solitary activity, sometimes involving browsing Internet sites of interest. Some reported that the novelty of the Internet had worn off, though they recognised its continuing utility.

The Protheroes and the Swaines each had a PC unused in a cupboard. In the case of the former, the purchase had been instigated by their son, but they had found it unduly complex. They had dismantled it to decorate a room, since when it had remained upstairs in a cupboard. John Swaine had bought a package about a year ago, to help the children with their education. It included the hardware and some educational software, including an atlas, a medical encyclopaedia and the *Encyclopaedia Britannica*, but had been little used, and had been needing repair for some months. Both cases would seem to suggest that 'the digital divide' is not simply a material phenomenon, but concerns expertise or cultural knowledge.

Even in our households that used their PC, the PC remains a hidden medium. In all the households with a PC and Internet access, the PC was in a bedroom, study, or other room away from the main living space – in contrast with radio or television. Although in their early days radio and television appealed to technically-minded men, they arrived in the living space – either the kitchen or the living room.[57] The PC and Internet, by contrast, are characterised by greater spatial and social fragmentation and isolation. We found that using the PC was often solitary and found no instances of its use as a group activity. In the Riley household the PC is in the bedroom.

> Richard and I went into the bedroom to use the PC. Richard booted it up, which took a short time. The family is on AOL and bought their PC at PC World as a package, with scanner printer and digital camera and software. "We had it for just under a thousand pounds, which we thought was reasonable for these things. The photographic software [Photoshop] is really good and the camera as well, I use that a lot."
> *Richard Riley, 6 January 2002*

Mark James uses his PC for work and provides an insight into why the PC has not found a place in the living room.

---

57 Shaun Moores (1988) "'The Box on the Dresser": memories of early radio and everyday life', *Media, Culture & Society*, vol. 10, no. 1, pp. 23–40; Tim O'Sullivan (1991) 'Television memories and cultures of viewing, 1950–65' in John Corner (ed.) *Popular Television in Britain: Studies in Cultural History*, London, British Film Institute.

"Dwi'n defnyddio laptop ac e-bost ar gyfer gwaith, mae'n rhaid cael o ar gyfer gwaith …. Mae'n dda defnyddio e-bost a stuff hefyd." ["I use the laptop mainly for work and email, it's essential for my work … it's good to use email and stuff as well."]

He shut the laptop, folded down the screen and put it conveniently to one side, leaving space for reading or writing.

"Gwell gen i'r laptop, mae'n dipyn mwy defnyddiol ac yn fwy addas dyddiau'ma. 'Dwi ddim eisiau rhywbeth sy'n wneud llwyth o bethau 'dwi ddim yn defnyddio. 'Dwi'n defnyddio'r Wê yn anaml; felly 'dwi angen rhwybeth ysgafn, ac yn siwr 'dwi ddim eisiau ryw beiriant mawr sy'n cymryd fyny hanner ystafell. Mae PCs yn rhy fawr i ddweud y gwir, mae nhw'n cymryd lle." ["I prefer the laptop, it's a bit more functional and that suits me more, these days. I don't want anything that does a million things I won't use. I hardly use the Internet; so I want something portable that suits my needs … I also don't want a bulky PC that takes up half my room. PCs are too big really, they're a bit of a waste of space."]
Mark James, 7 January 2002

The Addey and Rowlands household had Internet access in their living room, via NTL, but this did not really work out.

"It never works. It worked for a while but not for ages now. Anyway, without the keyboard you can't get all the interactive features anyway. Plus you're limited to certain websites. It's crap. If you want the keyboard and wider access you have to pay more each month."
Paul Addey, 15 October 2001

Rhian Powell illustrates how PC usage blurs the boundaries between public and private by shifting the boundary between home and work.

"I also use the PC for work. I email figures to my desk each night ready for the morning, or any work I need on my desktop for the next day. It's easier than sitting at the office doing horrendous amounts of overtime. The home computer makes my working day shorter at the office, but [it] does tend to encroach on my personal life."
Rhian Powell, 28 December 2001

The use of the PC in the home primarily for work goes some way towards understanding its absence from predominantly social or recreational space in the home.

"I'm not really the type of person that likes to sit in front of the screen when I get home, I get enough of that at work."
Rhian Powell, 28 December 2001

We found a relatively low usage of the Internet for surfing. Most avoided surfing because of the costs of being online.

They told me that they do not tend to surf, as it takes too long and costs too much to surf for fun. They have an Internet Service Provider (ISP), but do not have free surf time, so they are constantly vigilant about the cost of being online (2p a minute). They told me that they tend to know what they're looking for before they go online and tend to use it only for specific work-related sites. Ieuan told me that this way worked out less expensive than paying for a monthly Internet subscription.
James household, 29 August 2001

Others have opportunities to use the Internet elsewhere.

"I don't really use it at home because we've got access at school. It's free at school so why pay at home?"
Dafydd Lewis, 14 December 2001

Use of the Internet for surfing is prohibited in their school, so is the use of chat rooms and messaging, but most of the children use these at school at some point during the day. Their use of the Internet and email seems to be part of a school subculture, and a means to 'get one over' on the teachers. Dafydd told us what sites he visited most often.

"Stuff we're not supposed to really; adult sites most of the time, sometimes game sites where you can play games online ... these are like stupid games like ten pin bowling which you can play at the same time, you can play them on sites like netbabyworld.com, that's a good one."
Dafydd Lewis, 14 December 2001

Another way of saving money is to take advantage of free Internet trials and to change ISP quite often, to have free surf time. The consumer plays one company off against the others and takes advantage of their introductory offers, before cancelling.

He connected to the Internet via Freeserve, although his father also had access through BT. "Rwyn newid darparwyr gwasanaeth yn debynnu ar pwy sydd a'r cynigion gorau, neu treialon am ddim." ["I tend to switch between service providers depending on who's got the best offers, or free

trials."]
Mark James, 7 January 2002

"We change ISPs now and again if they have a free trial. AOL's about the easiest to use and they give you tons of links to good sites."
Brian Powell, 28 December 2001

The Powell household demonstrated the greatest use of the Internet for surfing sites as a form of entertainment.

Gareth was on the Internet and was looking at the *Lord of the Rings* website www.lordoftherings.net to view a trailer of the film. He was showing his father who had yet to see the film, but was tempted to go. Gareth had found the site using the Google search engine, which they have on their 'favourites' list. They have the new AOL 7 package, which provides them with a trial 100 free hours on the Internet.

"I used to go to the Napster site, but we had BT then and they cut you off after two hours, AOL don't do that, so I've had a few albums down off some illegal warez [cracked programmes/software] sites like musikum.com, that's a good one."
Gareth Powell, 16 January 2002

Others have cooled off over time. Having once used it a lot for surfing, for Rhian Powell the novelty has worn off.

"When we first got the Internet we used it all the time. I don't so much now, but I have ordered books through amazon.com and checked out cheap flights and cars, that kind of thing. I can take it or leave it, I'm really not that taken with it."
Rhian Powell, 16 January 2002

Some households preferred not to surf for too long because they did not like the risks involved in being logged on for extended periods of time. The Powells were worried about downloading viruses and illegal programmes.

"I don't like him having the machine on all night. I know it's free but I like someone to be in front of the machine when we're logged on, it might pick up a virus, crash, get hacked, anything, if you leave it connected all night. I have all my work and financial files on it and I've heard some horror stories at the club about other users scanning your files when you're on some of these illegal sites. Anyway you don't know when it might be traced on some of these sites. I'd prefer if he stayed away from some of the sites,

but I won't put a bar on it, he's old enough to be sensible."
Brian Powell, 16 January 2002

Most households used the Internet sparingly, for something specific – such as ordering goods, online banking or booking holidays. The Rileys find all the relevant websites they need on their AOL homepage without the need to navigate the complexities of the Web.

"I'm only used to some of the programmes on here, and some of them, well I never use and wouldn't know how. We don't play games, or surf the Web really."
Richard Riley, 6 January 2002

A major use of the Internet was to conduct research, to search for information – a new form of activity, or an enhanced and extended version of previous ways of doing something similar. With the Internet, markets are made more perfect, as choice is enhanced and consumers empowered.

He connected to the Internet and the email was sent. I asked him about the types of sites he had visited lately, about his 'favourites' and 'history'. He showed me his Internet 'history', which contained visits to their Internet banking, to the Ford Focus website and a recent visit to amazon.com, the online bookshop.

"I tend to go for the links on the AOL homepage, they've got a 'best of the Web' section and links to BBC news sport, shopping, weather, television guides and search engines – the lot. As I say, I don't surf, because most of what I'll ever need is listed here [the AOL homepage], you've got shopping, tesco.com, WH Smith, Argos. I use yell.com for telephone numbers quite a bit, and of course, we have just started doing Internet banking. That suits me, because I hate having to go to town to check my balance or set up direct debits. It's useful now, but at the start I was a bit sceptical about using it."
Richard Riley, 6 January 2002

Most people expressed concern at buying online and giving credit card details, but most had received good service on the Internet and would use it again. Mark James buys books online and recently searched for and booked tickets on the Internet for flights to New York.

"I got them from lastminute.com, I booked the accommodation by using Lycos I think it was and just typing in 'budget hotels in New York'. I found

a place which showed pictures on a map, I booked it through email with them, it was easy to be honest. I was a bit apprehensive at first, you know, because it wasn't face-to-face, but it worked out fine."
Mark James, 7 January 2002

Richard Riley has bought online, although his wife would never do so.

"Julie wouldn't dream of paying online, although we did buy some presents for Christmas on the Argos website."
Richard Riley, 6 January 2002

Others, like Brian Powell, seem completely at ease with online shopping.

"I sometimes surf the Web, mainly for online auctions, yesterday I ordered some new golf gloves on ebay.com. You can get some bargains if you look carefully enough."
Brian Powell, 28 December 2001

All of our households use either their service provider's links or well-known search engines to find what they want. Online shopping seems gradually to be becoming a more accepted form of shopping, with a growing confidence in our households. It is clear that they shop on the Web mainly at established high-street names.

Email

Email is used to cement long-distance relationships, and it is also used as a casual and informal means of communication with one's social circle. Email was used either to supplement local social networks, or to renew or maintain long-distance friendships. The Lewis boys use email and MSN Messenger to enhance their social life. Their very local use contrasts with the wider communication that is facilitated by these media.

"I use email in school, but I mainly send them to people I'm in school with. I don't use chat rooms, but we use Messenger in school, we use it to arrange to meet after school, or to tell the girls where we're going to be on Friday night or something. I don't know anyone on the other side of the world to contact, most of them live in the town and go to our school; we use it like text messaging on a mobile."
Dafydd Lewis, 14 December 2001

Others use email to contact distant family and friends at a lower cost than calling by telephone. Email might be seen as a less formal means of communication.

With the Powells, it is a way of checking up on their daughter's progress, without being overly intrusive.

"We keep in touch with Anna at university through email, she uses it quite a lot during the week, when she's at the library supposedly writing essays."
Rhian Powell, 18 January 2002

The Rileys bought their PC with email in mind. Email provides a link to their daughter overseas and is used along with the telephone. Rather than replacing the telephone for contacting relatives, it complements it, with some advantages. Its use resembles research findings regarding the early use of the telephone, to overcome isolation. Email allows this, but with the added advantage of temporal flexibility.

We were discussing their Internet and email use. They reiterated that they used it only to email their daughter, who they normally email or telephone (sometimes both) on Sundays when it is cheaper.

"We usually get in touch over the email during the week, but Julie likes to call her on Sundays, she hasn't been there that long ... I prefer the email because I can send pictures as attachments ... I'll show you." Richard opened up the machine and selected some recent digital photographs from his files. He uses Outlook Express in Windows 98 to write and send an email to his daughter. "I like to attach something for her to look at, even if it's just the dog and Julie together, it's nice."
Richard Riley, 6 January 2002

Mark James uses email rather differently, having separate work and personal email addresses.

"I've got a Hotmail account for all my friends, which I set up before travelling, I still use that and keep my new address for work. It's a good way of keeping work separate, otherwise my email gets clogged up with loads of junk mail."
Mark James, 7 January 2002

Email and the Internet mean that Mark can do more of his research from home, so he does not have to live near to his place of study, as would have been the case some years ago. Similarly his father communicates with his staff electronically so that he can work more from home.

Our research suggests that the PC has a considerable way to go before it becomes a feature of the living room (or that the living room has to change considerably before the PC becomes unobtrusive and acceptable in it). Use of the Internet is quite low, although its use for shopping is increasing steadily as households come to trust the new technology. Email as a practical tool has encouraged the greatest use, and indeed has stimulated the purchase of PCs. The use of home computers seems far from the life-changing experience predicted by some.[58] Generally their use is everyday and mundane, and the lure of the information superhighway is constantly weighed up against the costs and dangers. Confidence in the content of the Internet is linked to trusted names (mostly from the high street). Internet service providers act as shepherds for the newly initiated to the Web, with many of our households dependent on these to navigate the Internet. Apart from email and shopping, the Internet was used from home for work, to undertake research, to search for information (commonly to inform consumption decisions) and to make purchases. It remains to be seen whether each of these follows the trajectory of the television, telephone and VCR, which are now found in the vast majority of households, or whether each will have a smaller significance in domestic life, with a multiplicity of devices competing with one another for a place in the home. History shows us that these technologies rarely follow their predicted trajectory, and the computers that we found in cupboards testify to this possibility. What we found was far from both the virtual communities that are often referred to,[59] and the picture painted by postmodern theorists, of the Internet as a place and the possibilities afforded of free-floating virtual identities and activities.[60] Rather we found Internet and email use firmly located in a context, socially, biographically and spatially rooted.

---

58   For example, Nicholas Negroponte (1995) *Being Digital*, London, Hodder & Stoughton.

59   Howard Rheingold (1994) *The Virtual Community: Finding Connection in a Computerized World*, London, Secker & Warburg.

60   Sherry Turkle (1996) *Life on the Screen. Identity in the Age of the Internet*, London, Weidenfeld & Nicolson.

Chapter 4

Making sense of the households and their media

In this chapter we have used five analytical categories to make sense of our ethnographic data – temporal rhythms; domestic space; gender; spaces of identification; and the Welsh language. We have used these categories because of the particular interests of the media organisations that supported this research (for example, uses of EPGs and 888 subtitles), our own interests (particularly in new media technologies), and the literature (the work of researchers who have developed and deployed these categories productively in recent qualitative studies of media consumption). They have been selected and applied to the data because they seem to be a fruitful way of making sense of what we observed and were told. Our analysis is very much driven by our data, and the connections between that and our *a priori* knowledge and understanding.

Temporal rhythms

In this section we explore how media uses connect with temporal rhythms in households, how they slot into and shape the daily routines of households, and how they are used to order time. The media naturalise, stabilise and structure the day – for example, the radio in the early morning routine of most households or the ritual of the evening news.[61] Scheduling draws on and constructs such patterns of behaviour. Media use is shaped largely by the availability of time, by the time constraints experienced – so generation, or stage in the lifecycle, is a key

---

61   Paddy Scannell and David Cardiff (1991) *A Social History of British Broadcasting. Volume One, 1922–1939. Serving the Nation*, Oxford, Blackwell.

determinant of patterns of media consumption. As well as being constrained by time, the media are used to make time for oneself, to construct some boundary to prevent other people or activities from impinging on personal space. So our argument is not that time has ceased or been reconstituted by new media (nor, in the next section, that space has vanished), but that temporal arrangements within and beyond the home are undergoing a transformation, and the mass media are a key part of this process.

Media consumption is routinised and ritualised, but in the contemporary era in particular these routines and rituals are transforming. The VCR, of course, has been a means of disrupting or opting out of the flow of television, of breaking free from the constraints of broadcasters' schedules. With multi-channel television and 24-hour news, however, the disruption of flow has reached an entirely new level, with the fracturing of the constraints and structure with which broadcasting has been associated. In multi-channel households we found reduced usage of VCRs (due to more repeats and more channels) and a preference for rolling news, with individuals exercising greater control over viewing choice. Together these represent a profoundly different form of engagement with television.

First we examine typical temporal routines in several households and report the rituals that revolve around set programmes and schedules. We explore how different households' media routines are shaped by generation, or life-stage, and lifestyle.

We begin by comparing the flow of time in various households. Paul Addey and Christopher Rowlands, one unemployed and the other working part-time, have the time to hang around the house playing games and watching MTV.

> In the corner of the room facing the window, the Nintendo was on pause – and remained so for the duration of my visit. It appeared that the game (*Zelda*) was a semi-permanent fixture, available to play at any opportunity. Christopher was preparing to go to Port Talbot and Paul had the day off. Neither chose to go out into the sun – even though it was a really hot day. The flat was cluttered with empty plates and half-drunk cups of tea. A few guitars lay around and were frequently picked up and played with an ease and lack of concentration, often as a secondary activity to watching the television or having a chat. Paul made me a cup of tea and the atmosphere was relaxed and lazy, perhaps due to the heat of the sun. He asked if I had seen Radiohead on MTV2 and whether I liked their new single. I repeated 'no' on both counts, but said that I liked the band. Music is clearly a

reference point. Paul commented that MTV is usually the staple when their friends are around as it gives them a chance to "slag other bands off".
Addey and Rowlands household, 23 May 2001

Richard Riley retired recently and likes to spend his day tending the garden. He, too, has time on his hands during the day.

> I arrived to find Richard and Stella the dog in the back garden. Richard was cutting back the shrubs and bushes ready for them to grow again in the spring. The well-tended garden reminded me of an oil painting. Richard had some green beans from the garden and he also grows tomatoes. The frustrating thing for Richard, I suppose, is that, as the artist, he probably knows that he should not do any more, but he has so much time on his hands. The garden shed door was open and he put his clippers away. The dog spent the time running around the garden, occasionally coming to jump up on me. We went into the kitchen, where Richard was preparing potatoes and fish for their evening meal. All the vegetables were in the pans ready to go, before Julie came home at around 4.30 p.m.
> *Riley household, 6 November 2001*

Being retired, Richard (like the Protheroes) reads the broadsheet newspapers in greater depth and in longer continuous time spans. For them, reading the newspaper is more about 'passing time' than 'making time'.

Other households, generally those with young children, are much busier. John Swaine works various long shifts, leaving Michelle alone with the children.

> There had been an enforced change in working practices and John now had to work afternoon shifts for the foreseeable future – 3 p.m. to 1 a.m. rather than his night shift. This has meant that he sees much less of the children than he used to. Michelle preferred it when he worked nights, because it meant that he would see the children after school for a few hours before he would go to work. Now he only sees the children on Saturdays and Sundays, which has put more pressure on her during the evenings to spend time with the children, helping with homework, reading and so on. She says that it is difficult for her as a working mother to have no help at home during the evenings. She has to cook and clean, while the demands of the children for attention focus solely on her. They tend to "play up" more often now, because they know that John will only be there at the weekend.

The children continued to play with their toys and generally run around –

they hardly noticed the television at all. The children were having what Michelle calls "their mad half-hour", which lasted for at least an hour, during which time Michelle switched channels to BBC1 to watch *East Enders*.
Swaine household, 10 July 2001

Thus we see how – within constraints – time spent with the media becomes structured or routinised. Michelle Swaine's media routine focuses on the soaps.

I asked Michelle if she tended to watch any programmes regularly. Initially she told me that she does not get much time to watch television. Her daughter, however, protested, presenting a rather different picture: "You watch *Emmerdale* and *EastEnders* and *Coronation Street* all the time."

"Ssshhh Amy I'm talking. I do like the soaps and the kids will watch them with me, I like the news as well." We discussed the diaries. Michelle commented that she actually watches more than she thought and was surprised at the repetitiveness of her lifestyle – noticing that she had the same patterning every day. "Is this really my life?" she asked.
Swaine household, 31 October 2001

Karen Lewis is a single parent and works full-time, so has very little personal time.

"As I say I don't get much time to watch television, what with working and the family, I'm not really that bothered with it. The boys tend to watch it the most … I'm always worn out after work and by the time Hannah's gone to bed I'm not long after her up the stairs to be honest … I do have an hour to read in the front room, or sometimes watch the later news on HTV. I suppose reading is my time to myself, I'll have *The Western Mail* or the *Brecon and Radnor Express*, that comes out once a week, that's making time for me, otherwise I don't stop. I feel like I've got two full-time jobs most of the time, apart from the weekend when the boys are at their father's, then Hannah and me can do a lot more together."
Karen Lewis, 6 September 2001

Generation is another major factor in the availability of time and what it means. Dafydd Lewis describes a typical evening at home during the week.

"BBC2 is about the best after school. The programmes are aimed at my age group I suppose. I'll watch *The Simpsons* and *Star Trek* until the news comes on, then I'll probably watch BBC2 again after nine, 'cos there's

usually some comedy on like *I'm Alan Partridge*. Unless there's football on ITV, European Cup or Champions League, then I'll watch that ... Mam usually comes in to watch the 6 o'clock news on BBC1. I like the news as well, I never used to, but now I watch it quite a lot if I'm in."
Dafydd Lewis, 14 December 2001

Brian Powell also explained how media routines structure the evening for him, reflecting his lifestyle and personal taste.

"I will read most of the paper about this time of day, it's a quiet time before the house is full. I don't get a chance to read it in the morning, apart from on a Sunday ... I tend to watch a lot of sport on Sky Sports – golf and motor-racing mostly, I can't stand football ... I like to watch the television later at night, I always try to catch *Top Gear* when it's on and *Driven* on S4C."
Brian Powell, 1 November 2001

His son has a more leisurely lifestyle, which occasionally causes resentment or friction.

Gareth lay on the sofa watching *Neighbours* until Brian came home. Brian came in and told Gareth, "get your feet off the settee". He said to me, "He's like a bloody slug around here sometimes, bone idle, he sits there glued to the box. I bet he hasn't offered you a cup of tea or anything has he?"
Brian Powell, 1 November 2001

Media routines are thus associated with making time for oneself.

"I'll read half the paper in the morning before I go to work, I don't read it from cover to cover, and I don't bother with the sport in the back."
Michelle Swaine, 23 September 2001

"I hate Sundays, I can't get on with anything I want to do because the boys need feeding, the dog needs looking after and the horses need feeding in the night as well ... I don't get a minute to myself, it's better when they're all in work, then I get some peace, that's when I get a few hours in the afternoon to watch TV or read the magazines from the Sunday papers." She hardly has time to sit in the lounge and relax like Mr Daniels. When she is alone she might sit in the living room, but usually only late at night. "If I sit in the living room and watch TV the fire usually sends me to sleep. I'll wake up and then go to bed. I don't usually have time to sit down at

any other time in the day."
Elizabeth Daniels, 12 September 2001

During the week Karen Lewis reads *The Western Mail*, but it is not easy to fit this in.[62]

"Usually I'll have about 20 minutes to read it between 6 and 7 at night, that's when all the kids are doing something and they've all had their food ... the newspapers are a luxury, I can't make time to read them, I'll just skip through them when I can."
Karen Lewis, 20 September 2001

Like Rhian Powell, Karen Lewis shows how reading the newspaper is part and parcel of time and space for herself. For them, reading the newspaper is about making a few minutes or an hour for themselves, perhaps with a cup of tea. Thus much use of the newspaper is for brief periods – resembling somewhat the uses of bite-size 24-hour television news (discussed below). Reading the newspaper is regarded by many as something of a luxury. It is a form of media consumption that is perhaps more focused than the distracted nature of some television viewing by women – for example, Mrs Daniels.

"I suppose I do watch a fair bit [of television] but I don't really watch it properly, if you know what I mean ... I'll watch a bit of *Blind Date* and *Stars in Their Eyes* in the kitchen on a Saturday night."
Elizabeth Daniels, 20 July 2001

The media are also used to structure time, to keep one to time. In the Chandler and Thomas household we see how the television is fitted in and provides a measure of time, during one of the busiest times of the day. In the morning the news is used as a clock – like the radio in some households.

I arrived to find Stuart and Ann busily rushing around before leaving for work. They always got up exactly half an hour before they had to be in work. Stuart told me that this was because they live so near, that it takes them less than ten minutes to get to work. "You know what it's like, the nearer you live to work, the more time you think you've got in bed." Both

62   Broadly, our findings confirm Morley's categorisation of male television viewing as concentrated or focused, and female television viewing as involving multi-tasking and concurrent talk, and contradict Gauntlett and Hill's analysis of later British Film Institute surveys. See David Morley (1992) *Television Audiences and Cultural Studies*, London, Routledge; and David Gauntlett and Annette Hill (1999) *Television Living. Television, Culture and Everyday Life*, London, Routledge, in association with the British Film Institute.

were dressed and eating cereals in a rushed manner in the living room. BBC News 24 was on the television; neither really took much notice and continued to eat, looking up occasionally at the time shown on-screen. Ann ran upstairs to finish dressing and to brush her hair. They told me that they both like to watch the early news bulletins and that there are regular summaries every fifteen minutes on the BBC. They like to know what's been going on that night, or morning: it seems to give them some kind of orientation for the day ahead. Stuart "would normally listen to Radio Four in the kitchen, if I have time to spare and have a decent breakfast", but today he was very late.

Chandler and Thomas household, 5 July 2001

VCRs have long been a means whereby individuals and households have temporally opted out of media schedules to structure their own routines, rather than have them determined by broadcasters. The media in this context can be seen as being used to capture or shift time.

Following *EastEnders*, the children used the VCR to watch *Party in the Park*, a pop concert held that Sunday in London, in aid of The Prince's Trust. During the video, both children sat and watched quietly as some of their favourite artists performed. Since my arrival, this was the quietest time in the household. Amy sang along with Geri Halliwell, while Christopher sat passively with a toy car, his gaze fixed to the screen. Amy had operated the VCR herself to select and play the video. Michelle had no objections to her doing this as she had recorded it for the kids on Sunday for them to watch at a later date. The children know how to use the VCR to play videos, but do not know how to record using the timer. Michelle told me that she recorded it for them, because she happened to come across it while flicking through the channels.

Swaine household, 10 July 2001

The James family discovered some of their own home recordings, demonstrating a rather different use of the VCR to time shift, in this case to provide a link to the past.

Ieuan was in his study working for the coming school week. Mark and Gwyn had been watching an old VCR recording of them playing rugby. Mark told me, "we were looking to see what was on the tapes, we found this old one didn't we Mam and you wanted to watch it".

Lucy said, "I do like to see the old videos of the boys, I'd thought we'd lost

113

this one." She seems to like to mother the boys, even though they are in their late twenties and early thirties, but they do not seem to mind, or get embarrassed. We watched the footage of the boys playing rugby in a seven-a-side tournament. The video was fast-forwarded to "the good bits", as Gwyn called them. In many respects we had a potted history of the family right there. It seemed an almost idyllic family life on a Sunday. Gwyn commented, "it's not like this all the time you know, we're usually arguing over what's on".

James household, 7 January 2002

We have described, in the case of the Rileys' contact with their daughter in Canada, uses of the Internet, and email in particular, to connect with distant others without the problem of different time zones – in a way that is instant and does not require temporal synchronicity. This is another way in which media bring people together – one which we found in almost all of our households, albeit in different ways.

Christopher was making an effort to clean the flat before Sam, his girl-friend, arrived. He arranged the DVD and video remote control beside the television remote on the small coffee table in front of the settee. It seemed that they would be used during the evening. He said that he likes to stay in with Sam because they see very little of each other; so he prefers time alone with her, whereas in pubs or clubs they get no chance to catch up with one another or to talk in private. The media complement this wish to have a close and relaxed time with Sam, away from the distractions of his friends.

Christopher Rowlands, 17 June 2001

Household routines focus very much on key broadcasts, such as evening news bulletins, serial dramas or soaps. All of our households have regular programmes that they tune into at certain times of the week – but this is changing, notably with the news. With the availability of multi-channel television, more and more households watch 24-hour news, in bite-size chunks. These households find that 24-hour news and multi-channel television have released them from the temporal constraints of broadcasting, providing an instant, always-available service. In these households the regularity of news and the repetition and greater choice of films and programmes decrease the urgency to be in front of the television at scheduled times, disembedding media use from the constraints of scheduling. In multi-channel households, we found much less concern to record programmes on the VCR. The cyclical and diverse nature of multi-channel television has thus eroded the rituals associated with terrestrial television. The viewer feels more empowered with multi-channel, digital and interactive capabilities.

Mark James no longer has to sit up late to watch a programme, or even to set the VCR to record it. Television has become more convenient and user-driven.

> "With the guide I don't have to use the video, because I can see when Sky are showing a film again ... Sky rotate the films, so if you've got work the next day, you don't have to stay up late, 'cos you know you'll catch it again."
>
> *Mark James, 30 August 2001*

The cyclical nature of cable and satellite television tends to suit households with a busy lifestyle.

> "I like the fact that we have the 24-hour news. I don't get to see the evening news that often, so I can switch on and get a summary whenever I like."
>
> *Rhian Powell, 1 November 2001*

> "I usually turn Sky News on when I get home for the headlines. Because we normally get back at different times, Rhian and myself will switch to the news when we feel like it because we normally miss the teatime news, or are too busy doing the accounts or paperwork."
>
> *Brian Powell, 1 November, 2001*

It provides greater flexibility and greater opportunity for meeting preferences as and when they are felt.

> The James' were settling down to watch a film on television. Ieuan wanted to watch the news headlines before the film. Gwyn obliged and switched to Sky News. After about 15 minutes Ieuan said, *"Diolch, Gwyn, dw i'n hapus rwan"* [Thank you, Gwyn, I'm happy now]. Gwyn switched to *K2*, a film on Sky Movies that they all watched together.
>
> *James household, 7 January 2002*

Television has become 'on tap' regardless of the time of day. Bite-size news and the repetition of programmes mean that the media no longer punctuate the day but, rather, become the background against which the day is set. The media day unfolds in real time, in a less synchronic way than before. This diachronic process of emergence has important implications for how we understand relationships with the media. Not only do the media now present the world as it happens and events as they unfold, they also blur the boundaries between the consumer and the subject (in the case of television, between the viewer and the viewed). Some individuals seem to get deeply involved with the real-time process of emergence offered by global, real-time, around-the-clock television.

The events of the eleventh of September unfolded in real time in the living rooms of several of our households, demonstrating profoundly the instantaneity that characterises much of the modern media. Mrs Daniels discussed how it had affected her.

> "Everyone I've met is talking about it. I had a phone call at home, to switch on the television, as I did the other plane flew into the building, it was like watching a film, I didn't believe it at first. So I just watched the news as it happened, I can't believe they filmed there with all that going on."
> *Elizabeth Daniels, 12 September 2001*

Mrs Daniels watching the terrorist attack unfold as it happened is a graphic example of a temporal process of emergence facilitated by 24-hour television news.

In the process is a shift in the distance between viewer and viewed. Members of some households displayed what might be described as voyeuristic tendencies, as illustrated by Ann Thomas watching *Big Brother*.

> We returned an hour later to find Ann watching live coverage of *Big Brother* on *E4*. She commented that she preferred the live coverage, rather than the summary show on Channel 4, because you get to see the nuances of the interaction. She felt that this was a better way to understand the relationships between the members. She went on to say that she found it interesting to watch "people forming false relationships". She thought that it was "a symptom of society that the media can create celebrities out of complete strangers simply by exposing the public to them 24 hours a day".
> *Ann Thomas, 2 July 2001*

This engagement with the process of emergence has stimulated intense use of the media as an information source. Mr Daniels' priority when he arrives home is to switch to the news channels on Sky.

> Mr Daniels was positioned so that he could watch the television in the other room. Sky News was showing and he ate with the news bulletin as a background. His main source of news in the evening is BBC News 24, the Bloomberg Channel (for financial news) and sometimes Sky News.

"I don't watch any other Sky channels apart from the news and financial channels."
James Daniels, 20 July 2001

His consumption of 24-hour news is not, however, at the expense of newspapers – as we reported in Chapter 3, Mr Daniels is an avid reader of quality broadsheets. This contrasts with another multi-channel household (the James') where 24-hour news is used instead of national newspapers, except occasionally on Sundays.

The media are used to make time, to pass the time and, importantly, to construct a sense of time – for example, with the evening news. However, the role of the media in constructing senses of time seems to be decreasing with new technologies. Households with multi-channel television and the Internet have greater freedom regarding the time at which they can consume their media. Multi-channel television is more agent-driven, with users more proactive. This is a direct threat to the traditional role of the morning newspaper, the evening news and the weekend sports results, for example. All of these form pillars of household media rituals and yardsticks by which one might measure the passing of time. We are seeing the gradual decaying of these pillars. Bite-size media consumption seems to chime with the busy modern lifestyle, although it co-exists with the almost religious regular viewing of favourite broadcasts and television shows, or the reading of a preferred newspaper. Thus time has become more fluid, though it remains patterned and routinised.

With regard to 24-hour television and news, engagement with developing stories can become captivating, giving the viewer a more proactive role in the consumption of the news, rather than the paternalist or traditional form of addressing the nation at a given time, informing the public of events. The news has become more globally focused and more accessible at the same time. Multi-channel television has thus empowered users to control when and where they use the media.

Individuals still shift time and construct their temporal routines around the media. The importance of the idea of emergence, however, is that, whereas we might have measured the passing of time in some synchronic or snapshot form, we now see a diachronic process of engaging with news, events and programmes as they happen. Viewing in real time not only shrinks space and time, but also the distance between subject and object, between the viewer and what is viewed.

Domestic space

Next we examine the relationship between uses of the media and household space, which relates to consensus and conflict in the domestic environment. We shall discuss how household members use the media and household space to exclude or to link with others. Such practices are closely connected to notions of private and public space within the home, space in which household members can spend time alone or can come together. We shall show how the media fit into and create the space people use in their homes, and also how the uses of space are being transformed by the new media.

In most of our households the living room is the main public space where family and friends come together to use media devices. Such use, commonly, is patterned or ritualistic, as media routines have developed. Members of the James household enjoy each other's company and like to spend time together when they can. The following is a snapshot of their living room.

> Near the television was a large stock of videos and audio CDs covering an eclectic mix. The stereo, television, PlayStation and Sky receiver all occupied this corner space, indicating that this room functioned as a focal point for family 'get together time' and that it was used frequently for this purpose. Family games such as Pictionary and Who Wants to be a Millionaire were easily visible, and looked well-used. Mark said that he had been playing Millionaire with his girlfriend and the rest of the family the night before. As a family, they come together for leisure and relaxation by using the television or video as a family-time occasion. It brings them together despite their otherwise very busy and separate lives outside the home. They seem very close and relaxed in each others' presence, and the family and time together are important to all of them.
> *James household, 14 September 2001*

Nicola Davies and her daughter, too, use the living room as a space and television as an activity for bonding.[63]

> "I usually get home [referring to her mother's house] before *EastEnders*, so I'll watch that. I stay in most of the time with Lou, sometimes my mother will have her, but I hardly go out any more. I can't afford it and it's too much hassle half the time. I can't be bothered. We stay in and watch

---

[63] The 'affiliation' of the affiliation/avoidance tactics that James Lull found employed by household members in using the media and domestic space. See J. Lull (1980) 'The social uses of television', *Human Communication Research*, vol. 6, no. 3, pp. 197–209.

EastEnders together, we really like it. We sit on the settee together with a big bag of crisps, I like that. It's nice after not seeing her all day. It gives us a chance to spend time together."
Nicola Davies, 29 November 2001

In some households, high levels of technology allow for evening entertainment at home using a whole range of different devices in one space. As we have discussed, in some households living rooms have become more complex media centres, often with multi-functioning media devices, which take considerable skill to operate. The Lewis boys' living room is an example.

The television was linked via a cable to a hi-fi and speakers and on the shelves were row after row of videos and books. The PlayStation and VCR sit under the television in a cabinet with three shelves. The room is relatively small and square, with sofas hugging the walls in front and to the right of the television set. The PlayStation games are always out of their covers and are stacked on top of each other in a small tower of CDs. The layout of the room reflected its use as a room for the boys to spend time watching television and videos and playing the PlayStation.
Lewis household, 14 September 2001

Thus, as another researcher found, the presence or absence of different types of 'specialised' space in the household gives rise to particular forms of media use.[64]

The Addey and Rowlands household stages regular boys' nights in with the games console, DVD and home cinema system functioning as major attractions for their friends – as we discussed in Chapter 3. Typically they might spend most of the evening playing *Quake Arena* together and drinking tea.

The living room is used to entertain and to reinforce social relationships, which is often facilitated by uses of the mass media. It is not just new technologies that are used to create such social spaces. Nicola Davies and her friend hired a video cassette to facilitate their girls' night in.

Nicola was there with her friend Hannah and Hannah's young son of about 2. Louise and the boy (Jamie) were sitting in front of the television watching Disney's *Hercules* from the VCR. Nicola and Hannah were sitting in the kitchen at this time at a small table having a glass of white wine while Hannah was smoking with the backdoor ajar, "to let the smoke out". Nicola

---

64   James Lull (1990) *Inside Family Viewing: Ethnographic Research on Television's Audiences*, London, Routledge.

told me, "tonight we're having a girls night in … We've got a video for later from Hannah's house and we'll probably order a pizza". Hannah is one of Nicola's closest friends and she often comes over for the night. "Jamie sleeps here, if he's tired we don't wake him, they'll stay over … we have a couple of bottles of white wine from KwikSave down the road."

I asked them about how the night would be spent in a little more detail and whether it was a regular thing. Nicola said "it used to be every week, now it's every two weeks, it's the only time we see each other, apart from speaking on the phone … the kids entertain themselves either watching videos, or in Lou's bedroom playing. It gives us a chance to catch up and have a few drinks for a change!"

"I've got *Shrek* from the video shop", Hannah told me, "I haven't seen it yet and the kids can watch it, if they're still awake later."
Nicola Davies, 11 January 2002

These examples illustrate how the media are used in the home as a means of facilitating social interaction. We also observed the opposite, exclusionary practices, subtle and less subtle, to create and demarcate private and personal space in the household. We observed many instances of one family member taking control of, or dominating, household space. Lucy James reported how one particular television programme created space for her.

"When *Bad Girls* is on, they know to give me my space for an hour or so. They know that it's my time to watch what I want in the living room."
Lucy James, 7 January 2002

With Mr Daniels, it is usually while he watches the news in the living room. The living room, with the multi-channel television, is primarily his space.[65]

Mr Daniels tends to switch on BBC News 24 first thing in the morning before he goes to a work-site or the yard, and always when he comes home at about 6.30 p.m. (except on Sunday, his day off). "On Sundays I'll listen to Classic FM and Radio Cymru in the morning while I read the papers." Mrs Daniels interjects: "you sleep all afternoon after dinner, you don't watch anything." Mr Daniels defended himself by saying, "I have one eye

---

65   This is an extreme variant from Bausinger's typology of television viewing as an excuse for *not* communicating with fellow family members at all. See Hermann Bausinger (1984) 'Media, technology and daily life', *Media, Culture & Society*, vol. 6, no. 4, pp. 343–351.

open to watch the television and the other to rest."
Elizabeth and James Daniels, 21 July 2001

In the evening *Heartbeat* on HTV was on in the kitchen but not being watched as Mrs Daniels cleared up. The boys were going out. "I'm glad to get some peace in here. Just me and the dog. He's [James] off out later with his cronies so I'll have a sherry and sit in the living room."
Elizabeth Daniels, 12 September 2001

John, the son, says that visitors are not usually invited further than the kitchen because he [Mr Daniels] is usually asleep after dinner and no-one wants to go in there and hear his snoring.
John Daniels, 23 September 2001

Mrs Daniels said that the living room was his [Mr Daniels'] domain. The boys only go in when there's something they really want to watch or if he's gone out for the evening with his friends. Mr Daniels has his papers, reading glasses, slipper and zappers ("gadgets", he calls them). He puts his feet on the coffee table. The two boys come in and out, picking up papers that are not in use. It strikes me as rather like a lion's lair.
Daniels household, 21 July 2001

It was remarkable that, in his absence, the boys filled the power vacuum and, if both were present, vied with one another to control the choice of programme. With them, programming was more entertainment-based – sports and films – and the living room thus became, if only briefly, an entertainment rather than an information space. In the living room Mr Daniels usually sat, and often lay, on one of the two settees. Although others entered the room and shared the space, it was very much controlled by him. In his living room, probably like at work, Mr Daniels is in control and dealing with information. He would often switch over from what others were watching when he arrived home without asking, or would herd them out of the living room so that he could get some peace. There was complete acceptance of his power or right to do this. We saw him switch over to the news in order to empty the room, then switch to another channel once he had achieved this.

John watched *Clockwork Orange* on Sky Box Office. Mr Daniels arrived home just as the film finished. John said this was fortunate because he would have switched the television over to the news.
Daniels household, 31 August 2001

Thus although it was a space for entertainment in Mr Daniels' absence, the living room was not a place for the family to relax.

The kitchen, on the other hand, was the zone for face-to-face interaction, and the place where people 'popped in'. It was also the space that Mrs Daniels established as her own.

> Mrs Daniels was in the kitchen. "I usually sit in here on a Friday night. Someone usually calls for a drink if they're passing, we'll sit in here. James won't have people in the living room when he comes home from work, he'd probably throw them out … It's easier to be in here, if he's sleeping or watching the news I prefer to be in here, I can watch what I want then. Usually I have a stool next to the table. To be honest, I like to be in here having a bit of peace … I'll have it [the television] on the worktop when I'm cooking, normally just for the HTV News at teatime. It's on in the background normally, but things like *Blind Date, Don't Try This at Home* …"
> *Mrs Daniels, 1 December 2000*

As Brian Powell saw it, particular household members 'owned' different rooms.

> "The living room is my space in the house. Gareth's got his room and June's got the rest of the house, I've just got the lounge and the garage."
> *Brian Powell, 28 December 2001*

John Swaine, because of his shift work, does not control the living room most of the time. On weekday evenings the living room and the television are controlled by Michelle and used mainly by the children, who dominate the living room. At the weekend, however, John tends to have control of this space – for his consumption of sport, a common basis or reason for fragmentation in households.

> "My Dad always watches sport and then we go upstairs."
> *Amy Swaine, 23 October 2001*

> "We usually leave the room when the football's on, Christopher usually watches it as well, but me and Amy usually go upstairs or go out. I usually stick to my programmes."
> *Michelle Swaine, 23 October 2001*

As well as male adults commonly asserting control over the living room, we found sibling rivalry over space, with ensuing conflict. Dafydd Lewis attempted to express his dominance in the household, but comes into conflict with his brother.

In such situations Karen, their mother, has to exercise her power over both of them.

"We argue most of the time, but never real fighting. He tends to watch what I'm watching most of the time and if he doesn't like it, tough. He usually just sits there quietly, well we both do. We sort of sit here and don't really watch what's on half the time, it's just something to do. We'll usually sit through loads of rubbish until something good comes on."
Dafydd Lewis, 14 December 2001

"Rhodri will want to play the PlayStation, while Dafydd will want to watch the television. Dafydd usually gives in to Rhodri, but it does cause friction. Sometimes I'll put my foot down if there's something I really want to watch or listen to, but not very often. Sometimes I'll have to settle some argument over who wants to listen or watch something, then I'll just switch it off altogether."
Karen Lewis, 20 September 2001

Use of space relates, too, to generation – albeit in ways that cross-cut with gender. In the Lewis household Hannah and her mother eat at the table in the kitchen, whereas the (older) boys do not do so so much. They tend to eat their food in front of the television.

Media and space also intersects with time. The newspaper, for example, (if delivered) starts at the front door and moves to the kitchen or where breakfast is eaten. As the day progresses it moves to the living room, perhaps to be found on the floor or the arm of a comfortable chair. In other words, it follows household activity through space as the day progresses – in some cases returning to the kitchen at particular times.

The emergence of new technologies (digital television, DVD and games consoles) seems to be leading to greater use of the main living spaces for the collective use of mass media. In households with multi-channel television, games consoles and DVD players, we found the household spending a considerable amount of time together in the living room. This greater sharing of living space might be linked to the high cost of this emergent technology and hence its absence (as yet) from the kitchen and the bedroom. (Or it might be, of course, that it is because households that come together in this way have acquired the new technology.) Households with multi-channel television have only one receiving device, so it occupies a central place in the social life of the household (as we explored in Chapter 3). With time, multi-channel television may reach further into the household and be a part of fragmented media use. For now, however, technical and economic constraints mean that multi-channel television is generally available only in the living room, in effect forcing household members into one space.

Conflict over space often led to some household members retreating to other spaces as a counter strategy, establishing private space of their own. Most of our houses had a rich distribution of media devices in separate spaces, albeit with the highest concentration in the living room. Karen Lewis describes the spread of media devices in her home and the fragmentation of the family into privatised spaces.

> "All the children have a television in their rooms, the boys have videos in each of their bedrooms. There are two televisions downstairs, one of them is only used to watch videos and to play the PlayStation. There's another TV in the living room and a small radio in the kitchen and the boys have hi-fi systems in their rooms. There's a PC with the Internet in the study [on the second floor]."
> *Karen Lewis, 10 July 2001*

Most members of the households in our research valued having their own space, the use of which often involved some use of the media.

By exploring fragmentation and uses of children's bedrooms we can begin to understand the formation of private space, the alternative to the public space of the living room. John Daniels' bedroom is a haven for his rock and motorcycle lifestyle.

> John was in his room, where he has a large collection of audiotapes, mostly rock and heavy metal from the early 70s and some 80s rock as well – including Hawkwind, Black Sabbath and ZZ Top. He has a Technics stereo hi-fi in his room, which would have been state of the art about ten years ago. His room is filled with bike magazines, mostly old issues of *Back Street Heroes*. There are cans of Heineken lying around by the bed. It seems that this area is used at the end of the night, for watching television with double vision. He had some rock music playing as I entered, and told me that he was about to take the bike out for a run, "I usually go out for a spin after work, I don't usually come back then until late. On weekends I'm usually away, I'll put a knapsack and tent on the bike and go off to a rally somewhere."
> *John Daniels, 12 September 2001*

Dafydd Lewis uses his bedroom for homework, listening to music and getting away from others.

> Dafydd's bedroom was bigger than I expected, with the amount of clothes on the floor that is typical of a teenage boy, and washing left in a pile for his mother to collect. "I listen to music up here while I'm doing my homework. I come up if Rhodri or Mam is in the downstairs lounge. I get more homework now I'm doing 'A' levels, so I need to have some space. Hannah is noisy sometimes as well, but the music drowns her out."
> *Dafydd Lewis, 25 October 2001*

Gareth Powell has no siblings at home to escape from, but he has a television, VCR and hi-fi in his bedroom.

> Most of his contact with the rest of the house during the evening is to eat and come down to take telephone calls from his friends. Gareth remained in virtual silence as his food disappeared in record time. As he finished, he left to go to his room. Gareth just seemed to want to have his own space. "I'm off upstairs to chill out and watch some TV, probably play some PS2 before I go out." Gareth spends most of his time in his room during the evening, although he does homework on the PC and sometimes surfs the Web. He has a collection of CDs, most on the floor, and stacks of car magazines (e.g. *Autocar*) piled around the bed and elsewhere on the floor. He has a Six Nations rugby poster on his door and one of the Stereophonics from a live concert he went to at Cardiff Castle. He has a PlayStation with G-Police, Tekken 3, and Final Fantasy 7.
> *Gareth Powell, 1 November 2001*

Bedroom space is not always totally outside the jurisdiction of parents, as the Powell family illustrates.

> Gareth was upstairs and we could hear Eminem playing on his hi-fi. Brian told me that he normally gets changed, rushes through his homework and then comes down for tea. "I don't know how he can concentrate on his homework with all that noise going on."
> *Powell household, 1 November 2001*

In the Daniels household we found a very similar situation.

> Mr Daniels shouted upstairs for Steven to turn his stereo down, "*Gad y swn na*" ['Shut that noise', in an abrupt and abbreviated form]. The two boys came in and out of the kitchen in order to put their motorcycles in their

garages. Mrs Daniels and I sat in the kitchen; Mr Daniels, on his arrival home, had turned off the television in the kitchen.
James Daniels, 21 July 2001

Particular rooms can be more or less 'public' at different times of the day. For parents of younger children, the living room can serve as private space later in the evening. Nicola Davies puts her daughter to bed and enjoys some time to herself in front of the television, either in the living room or the bedroom.

> "I tend to watch whatever's good on late at night, I'm normally just vegging anyway, so I don't really care. I'll switch the TV over on the flicker if I'm bored, sometimes there's nothing on, so I'll just watch any old thing." She tells me that she usually goes to bed quite early herself, but has a portable television in the bedroom and uses this to watch some late news or drama before she goes off to sleep. "I normally have the volume down low, so I don't wake her up."
> *Nicola Davies, 29 September 2001*

Another way of creating private space is by using personal headphones. They create private space anywhere in the household without physical separation.

> Occasionally Julie will watch *EastEnders*, during which Richard puts on his headphones to shut it out with some music. Alternatively, if Richard wants to watch something, Julie might go into the bedroom and use the PC to email their daughter in Canada.
> *Riley household, 6 November 2001*

Like the living room, the kitchen acts as a social and public space at some times but as a private space at others. The kitchen is often used as a first point of contact for visitors and as a place where family members come together in the mornings and when they come home.

> The kitchen area is where the Rileys like to sit and chat, sometimes reading the newspaper or listening to the radio. The radio usually accompanies any cooking that goes on. Both Richard and Julie like to cook and both like Classic FM because it has more music and less chat.
> *Riley household, 6 November 2001*

The kitchen is also used as a space where some household members retreat from the others. In many of our households, the kitchen was an area that women occupied while the living room was a male-dominated leisure sphere. Appropriation of the television and often the local newspaper in the kitchen was a recurrent feature of the Daniels, Powell, Riley and Protheroe households.

The Powell home is somewhat more egalitarian than that of the Daniels, with household space more shared, albeit shared somewhat unequally.

"Brian watches a lot of television when he's not at work, in the car or playing golf. He probably watches more than anyone else, with the sport and all the rest. If I'm in the living room later at night, then I get to watch something I like. I'm fine then, they can watch what they like, I'm either reading a book or catching up with the cleaning or ironing in the kitchen, although we do split the housework between us quite well."
Rhian Powell, 16 January 2002

Dominance and control of public spaces co-exists with expressions of individuality and the construction of different forms of personal or private space. The functions of particular spaces (such as the living room, bedroom and kitchen) are closely linked to uses of the media, which are important for the meaning or significance of a given room. We found a powerful gender divide between the living room and the kitchen in some of our households, with male dominance of the living room. We found collective or shared public spaces, with households coming together around a central hearth, but also fragmentation in the use of space and the media.

Gender

We have touched on gender as a key issue in patterns of media consumption at several points in this book – including the purchase and use of newspapers, television viewing styles, the availability of personal time and the control of space in the home. In this section we are not summarising or drawing together that material, but focusing on one important aspect of gender and media consumption: the relationship of women to new media technologies in the home. We found clear signs of ambivalence and resistance by women to digital television, EPGs and the Internet in most of our households. We should make clear that the women in our study are mostly older, and the adolescents were mostly male, so some of our findings regarding gender may in fact reflect the age, or generation, of our research subjects. Age, stage in the life cycle, class and other factors cut across and vary the nature of gender differences.

Early on, we found several mothers keen to emphasise their (and their household's) low levels of television viewing, and deprecating television for its negative impact on their children and family life. In most households mothers played down the role of television in their family's life, portraying a lower level of use by themselves and their families than transpired to be the case. Such a perspective was expressed recurrently and forcefully. Other researchers have found that negative feelings about television affects what people are willing to say about it – with frequent viewing often referred to with defensiveness or shame.[66] We found a gendered variant of this phenomenon. The overriding impression from mothers was that we should not regard household members as television addicts. This reflects the role of the mother as moral guardian of the family.[67] It translates, in some cases, in to a mistrust of new technologies, which are seen as damaging to the fibre of family life.

Lucy James was the strongest case of a mother referring to excessive use of television viewing as a bad thing. She clearly regarded herself as the moral guardian of the household. She was keen to stress that the family watches very little television, and distanced herself from the idea that television viewing was a major activity in the household.

> "TV has killed the art of conversation and has killed creativity … town children get bored much quicker and they need to be entertained. Country children on the other hand tend to entertain themselves."
> *Lucy James, 30 May 2001*

She said that she prefers encyclopaedias and reference books to the Internet.

In most households, the mothers displayed some ambivalence towards new technologies. In many cases this was about operating the VCR; in others, it was about disliking the PC, Internet and email. In multi-channel households it was voiced strongly regarding getting to grips with digital television, EPGs and remote controls. Lucy James displayed a general mistrust of new technologies as well as the television, describing herself as "a bit of a technophobe". She felt that the personal touch was being lost through an emphasis on speed and efficiency. She told us that she felt left behind and that the new technologies were aimed at the young. The family are online, although Lucy does not use the Internet.

> "It's killing the art of conversation, people are becoming less tolerant and rude because they're not talking face-to-face."
> *Lucy James, 14 May 2001*

---

66   Ellen Seiter (2000) *Television and New Media Audiences* Oxford, Oxford University Press.

67   David Morley discusses how the family is constructed or re-enacted in some idealised version – for example, in how we all smile for family photographs. It is lived, he says, as a series of hopes and fantasies. Women are crucial to the process, with much writing linking and blurring women, mothers and the home. See D. Morley (2000) *Home Territories. Media, Mobility and Identity*, London, Routledge.

Michelle Swaine also displayed a mistrust of the Internet, showing a tendency towards the moral guardian role, especially with regard to her children.

> "We were thinking of getting the Internet, but one of the girls in work was telling me that she had some really disgusting stuff downloaded to her. I think there's too much of that stuff on there."
> *Michelle Swaine, 10 September 2001*

Angharad Protheroe spoke about her feelings about having digital via a dish.

> "I don't particularly like the thing in the house or the dish; even though it's quite small ... Our son had it put in, just like the Internet, he talked us into it really, telling us how wonderful it was. I don't think it's that wonderful, but I suppose we're used to it now and we would miss it if we didn't have it when we're abroad."
> *Angharad Protheroe, 12 December 2001*

With the technologisation of living rooms that we have discussed, several women feel uncomfortable in their living rooms and find themselves struggling with the new technology. In households with multi-channel television we found local newspapers and television listing guides were used mostly by women – who preferred them to the EPG. Rhian Powell's attitude towards the new technologies in her home reveals much about how men and women see new media technologies in different ways.

> "They're just toys really for Brian and Gareth, I'll watch them if they hire a DVD. The digital TV is fine, as long as you don't get too into all the options and all the interactive stuff. I don't have the patience with the VCR, there's so many wires, Brian's hooked it up so it looks like a jungle behind the TV, I'm afraid to touch anything."
> *Rhian Powell, 18 January 2002*

Some of the women in our households have been slow to take-up and use some of the latest technologies and features in their homes, and tend not to use them that much.

Lucy James does not know how to use the EPG so buys the newspaper for the television guide for the coming week. Elizabeth Daniels normally watches terrestrial television because she finds the channels difficult to navigate. She feels that there is too much to choose from and that she would spend too much time flicking through to see what is on.

> "I don't bother with Sky unless someone else is watching it. I can't work

the thing, it's too complicated. I don't know what we had it for in the first place. James only sleeps in front of it anyway."
Mrs Daniels, 12 September 2001

"I'm getting to grips with it a lot more, I've had John show me how to work it, so that I can watch UK Food. I still go through the channels until I find it. The options and guides are just too much, they confuse me as much as anything. I know what I want to watch so I'll just switch to it. There's so much choice you'd be there forever otherwise … I've seen an advert for BBCi [BBC Interactive] on the *Walking With Beasts* programme. It's all a bit much really isn't it? Sometimes you want to watch TV without all this fuss. I've seen the adverts for *Who Wants to be a Millionaire* with the monkey, that looks interesting and you can play for a million through your television. I'd quite like to have a go at that, but I think you need a keyboard? On the whole, I'm quite happy with what we've got. I don't watch that much television on the whole, to really take that much of an interest in all these new gimmicks. Apart from UK Food now, I really don't watch that much Sky. I'll usually just have a portable on in the kitchen when I'm in there."
Elizabeth Daniels, 1 December 2001

Other are more engaged with the new technologies, but still display a general ambivalence.

"What's an EPG? Oh you mean the listings. Sometimes Geoff will use them to see what's on. Usually we switch to the news as I say, or flick through to see if anything looks good. I don't tend to use any of the features; I know sometimes that you can use the interactive control to participate in opinion polls on specific questions. You can use it to bid on the auction channel as well, but I haven't bidded – although it looks straightforward, I have terrible trouble getting it to work. We sometimes spend ages, as you know, trying to get the thing to operate. Geoff's not much better either, except he has less patience then me. It's his own fault, our son came around and talked him into getting Sky and linking it to the hi-fi speakers. It is so complicated to switch it, half the time we don't bother. The box keeps overheating I think and it doesn't work properly from time to time. I think we need a new one, or an engineer to come out … Really, I like to watch only a few things on television, so I don't bother that much with the guides."
Angharad Protheroe, 12 December 2001

Such approaches to new technologies confirm the findings of a range of research studies of gender and technology.[68] As to whether the profoundly gendered nature of contemporary new media technologies changes in the course of time, as it did with radio and television, would seem to depend on the development of a user-friendliness that at present seems lacking in VCRs, digital television and EPGs.

Regarding the more established technologies, we found a continuing divide in the use of the VCR, particularly in using its more complex functions. In this our findings confirm older studies[69] but contradict firmly recent research that found uses of the VCR to be no longer gendered, that found that women said that they are able to operate the VCR.[70]

Karen Lewis does not use the VCR to record very often, but knows how it functions well enough to set it without assistance.

> "If I'm going to miss this show [*The Blue Planet*, on BBC1] I'll set the video, it's really good and one of the few programmes I'll actually set time aside to watch, that's very rare for me!"
> *Karen Lewis, 20 September 2001*

Lucy James, however, has little idea of how to use the VCR to record programmes.

> "I never know how to stop the thing when it's recording, I forget it's on. The boys set it for me, I always forget, it drives Gwyn up the wall, doesn't

---

68   Studying the full breadth of technologies in the home, Jonathan Gershuny found that the more hi-tech a device, the more likely it is to be male-dominated in its use; James Lull found that many new media technologies were toys for men, with men performing the installation for their families. The responsibility gives men pleasure and control, as they perform for their families; Rogge and Jensen found 'the world of new media is principally a masculine domain'; Cynthia Cockburn has examined, historically and across cultures, how women are excluded from technology; and David Morley examined masculine and feminine forms of viewing and uses of the zapper. Morley discusses the gendered nature of socialisation in technological uses and competencies, and the symbolic as well as material nature of the culture of technology. See J. Gershuny (1983) *Social Innovation and the Division of Labour*, Oxford, Oxford University Press; J. Lull (ed.) (1988) *World Families Watch Television*, Newbury Park, CA, Sage; J.U. Rogge and K. Jensen (1988) in J. Lull (ed.) *World Families Watch Television*, Newbury Park, CA, Sage, p. 228; C. Cockburn (1985) *Machinery of Dominance*, London, Pluto; C. Cockburn and S. Ormrod (1993) *Gender and Technology in the Making*, London, Sage; D. Morley (1992) *Television Audiences and Cultural Studies*, London, Routledge.

69   Notably Ann Gray (1992) *Video Playtime. The Gendering of a Leisure Technology*, London, Routledge.

70   The difference may be due to different research methods. See David Gauntlett and Annette Hill (1999) *Television Living. Television, Culture and Everyday Life*, London, Routledge, in association with the British Film Institute. The BFI study is congruent with Sherry Turkle's work on computerphobia, which found that this is only a transitory phenomenon. See Sherry Turkle (1988) 'Computational reticence: why women fear the intimate machine' in Cheris Kramarae (ed.) *Technology and Women's Voices*, New York, Routledge.

it?" (Gwyn nods).
Lucy James, 7 January 2002

Rhian Powell calls her son if she needs anything recorded on the VCR.

> "The video's almost redundant these days apart from the odd episode of
> *EastEnders*. If I'm out and *The Western Mail's* got the listings for something
> I really want to watch, then I will phone Gareth from work to tape it. I'll
> watch it when I get home."
> *Rhian Powell, 18 December 2001*

In the Swaine household, too, using the VCR to record is a job performed by the
adult male.

> "It's John who knows how to use the video to select and record programmes
> in advance … I know how to play tapes and record the channel I'm
> watching, but setting the timer to record later is more tricky."
> *Michelle Swaine, 10 July 2002*

Nicola Davies, a single parent, simply does not use the record facility.

> "To be honest I can't even work the video to record properly never mind
> another machine … it's not because I'm thick or something, I just never
> really use it … I just press 'play' and 'rewind' or 'fast forward', that's it."
> *Nicola Davies, 11 January 2002*

In several of our households we found a counter process, whereby women who
felt excluded by, or unable to use, their new technologies focused on the more
traditional media – radio, local newspapers and terrestrial television.

> "I don't mind what we watch, as long as it's not too violent … I don't want
> to sit here with all hell breaking loose while I'm reading the paper."
> *Lucy James, 7 January 2002*

Most women had a set pattern of media use, which other members of the
household acknowledged and respected. In effect they asserted their domestic
power at certain times of the day or week, in the context of general male-dominated control of the media. Karen Lewis, like other mothers, has certain times of
the week when she gets to watch what she wants.

> "As I say I don't get much time to watch it, what with working and the
> family, I'm not really that bothered with it. The boys tend to watch it the
> most in the house … When Hannah's gone to bed, I'll watch a bit, we all
> tend to watch something really good, like *The Blue Planet* or *EastEnders*.

If the boys are here they'll watch it too, but usually they're out rugby or football training in the week."
Karen Lewis, 20 January 2002

"When Hannah goes to bed, sometimes Mam will come in and want to watch television. She likes *The Blue Planet* and *Walking with Beasts* on BBC1. The three of us will sit in here together, we don't really talk that much about things but we do spend time together; we all like those programmes anyway, so there's never any arguments."
Dafydd Lewis, 14 December 2001

Obviously, the gendered nature of media consumption relates to the sexual dimension of labour in the home. We found various arrangements, with a clear predominance of traditional patterns, exemplified by the Chandler and Thomas household.

I arrived just after Stuart and Ann finished work. The day had been very hot and the streets of Carmarthen had been quiet, with people setting off to enjoy the longest day of the year. On my arrival Ann answered the door and was busy making food for the two of them in the kitchen. Stuart was using the telephone upstairs, while Ann had music playing in the kitchen on the radio tape player. Ann seemed very busy in the kitchen adding frozen vegetables to a large wok on the stove. Stuart remained seated for the whole time, while *Neighbours*, the *Six O'Clock News* and *News of Wales* (both on HTV) were our background. Not once was he asked, or did he offer, to contribute to the food preparation during this time, which seemed strange for a young couple. The telephone rang next to Stuart on two occasions, which Ann answered, although the telephone was closer to Stuart. He seemed reluctant to answer the calls, which were both for Ann. Perhaps it is Ann who receives most of the telephone calls in the household.
Chandler and Thomas household, 21 June 2001

Mrs Daniels provides another clear example of how the place of media use is shaped by the sexual division of labour in the household.

Mrs Daniels was in the kitchen when I arrived, the small portable television on the worktop showing HTV Wales' teatime news. This formed the background to which Elizabeth Daniels juggled with a mix of saucepans and oven shelves in a professional manner. She sat on a high stool next to the worktop and had a drink, and we watched the television while chatting. The dog sat by Mrs Daniels attentively. She said that he was like a big baby

and that he (the dog) never leaves her alone. She said that most of her husband's workers come to visit and usually get a cup of tea and a bacon sandwich. Much like a farmhouse kitchen, Mrs Daniels spends a lot of her time in here, engaged in domestic tasks like ironing and washing, also cooking and filling her dishwasher. Having two grown up sons and a husband she said, "makes you realise that you have to do things yourself around here."
Elizabeth Daniels, 20 July 2001

She watches the local news and reads the local newspapers in the kitchen, while he reads the nationals and watches the national and international news in the living room. They exemplify *par excellence* the home as a site of leisure for the employed man, a place for relaxation after a day's work, for engagement in more focused television viewing. Mrs Daniels, meanwhile, reads the local newspapers in the kitchen.[71]

"We get the *Ammanford Guardian* as well as *The Evening Post* sometimes. I read them in the kitchen and I get more time to read them in the day than I do later on. I'll pick them up in Tescos in the afternoon when I'm shopping and I'll read them before anyone else."
Elizabeth Daniels, 21 July 2001

Mrs Daniels has the daytime to watch what she likes in the living room but has little time to do so. When she does, she mainly watches television in the kitchen. However, she has started to watch multi-channel television, having found a channel that interests her.

"Yes, this is a new channel that's just started in the last three weeks or so. It's a channel dedicated to food and cookery programmes during the day. I've watched it quite a lot since it began. I'll watch it during the day, although it mostly shows repeats of things like *Master Chef*, *The Naked Chef* and *Ready Steady Cook*. There are some good live items on there as well, but I suppose it's not everyone's cup of tea. I love to cook anyway, I find it a breath of fresh air from the news all the time and most of the rubbish on Sky."
Elizabeth Daniels, 1 December 2002

---

71   Janice Radway and David Morley are among those who discuss the home as a *workplace* for women. See J. Radway (1988) 'Reception study: ethnography and the problems of dispersed audiences and nomadic subjects', *Cultural Studies*, vol. 2, no. 3, pp. 359–376; and D. Morley (1992) *Television Audiences and Cultural Studies*, London, Routledge

In conclusion, we found that most women acted as the moral guardians of their households. Some displayed this through ambivalence towards new technologies entering the household and the perceived effect of these on household life. Most associated these new media technologies with masculine taste and saw them as predominately masculine gadgets. Other struggled to come to grips with the new media technologies, while a few used them with ease. We found that many of the women in our study made certain times of the day their designated times, and appropriated certain media and forms (local newspapers, local news and terrestrial television) as their domain. What emerges is the patterned use of particular media and technologies in specific household spaces – for example, the local newspaper being read in the kitchen.

Women's ambivalence towards new technology and their appropriation of more traditional media suggest that women are disenfranchised from the new technologies. They also suggest that women are taking control of the media with which they feel most comfortable (in the sense of technological competence). The more traditional or established media practices in households are being maintained by women.

Spaces of identification

First we look at the relationship between identity and locality, and at how the media are implicated in this. Specifically, we examine uses (or not) of the Welsh media, and how such use connects with the notion of Wales as an imagined community. We discuss the mix and match of local, national and global media, and how the local, national and global intersect in the everyday lives of our research subjects. Changes in such spaces of identification are transforming with new media and the resulting fragmentation. We examine the use of global communications to sustain a diasporic Welsh culture in one of our households; how dislocation from Welsh culture shapes the use of Welsh media in another; and an example of opting out of receiving Welsh television broadcasting in relation to a third household. Throughout we are adding detail and complexity to the notion that that mass media are resolutely national.[72]

We begin by examining how specific households identify with particular media texts in constructing a sense of self and place. Mr Daniels is clear, and stereotypical, about the readership of some major national dailies.

    "People who run the country tend to read *The Guardian*, whereas people

---

72   See H. Mackay (2004) 'The globalization of culture?' in D. Held (ed.) *A Globalizing World? Culture, Economics, Politics*, 2nd edition, London, Routledge.

who own the country read *The Times* and *The Telegraph*."
James Daniels, 14 July 2001

He also has strong views on who controls and benefits from Welsh broadcasting organisations.

"The BBC is a gravy train, it's jobs for the boys. S4C is like a Welsh mafia, run by academics ..."
James Daniels, 20 July 2001

Turning from media organisations to media forms, Angharad Protheroe likes the Welsh-language soap opera *Pobol y Cwm*, because of its association with her past experience of local everyday life.

"I'll watch *Pobol y Cwm* during the week and on Sunday if I've missed anything. I like it. Cwm Deri [where *Pobol y Cwm* is set] reminds me of home in the Amman Valley. Everybody knows everybody else's business. Yes I'll watch that religiously, but not a lot else I suppose."
Angharad Protheroe, 12 December 2001

Extremely strong support for *The Western Mail*, expressed in three of our households, was rooted firmly in senses of place and identity, of Wales and Welshness, and in an understanding of the core role of *The Western Mail* in this. In other words, while the newspaper's claim on its masthead to be 'the national newspaper of Wales' is undermined by its lack of significant circulation in mid and north Wales, this claim has considerable resonance among its readers.

"We felt like fish out of water without *The Western Mail*, we found that we couldn't do without it ... It's not just a newspaper, it represents Welsh culture. We've always had it even when we lived in London. We used to have it delivered even though the edition was then a day late. We had to have it."
Angharad Protheroe, 26 January 2002

Mr Daniels has been a reader of the newspaper for at least 50 years. He used to read it when he was at school; it was the newspaper of the household when he was growing up. "The family always read it, every farmer bought it, but it's gone to the dogs, I only read it out of loyalty ... I don't think its coverage of Welsh issues is of as good quality any more. It's become more Anglicised and appeals more to women these days." He will always support the paper because it's Welsh and will buy it if it were good or bad because it's a Welsh national paper. "I'll support it till I die. I'm cannon fodder for

them, but I don't suppose there's many like me left ... Three out of ten of my friends still read the paper." He does not like the pull-out supplements, which he finds irritating. He preferred the older layout, "as everything had a place". As he sees it, it was the newspaper that appealed to the masses in Wales in the past, regardless of their political slant. He attributes what he sees as a decline in the traditional support for the newspaper as the reason for its falling circulation. "The circulation was four times what it is now back in the 60s, but you had the support of the working classes in the Valleys then." With the additional support of the rural population in south-west Wales, the newspaper had a large share of the Welsh market. He felt the newspaper had left his generation behind, it had become feminised and focused more on the professional classes in south-east Wales. Although the newspaper covers local issues in Swansea and Carmarthen, its local focus has declined as it addresses the middle of the market. By this he meant that politically the newspaper was aiming somewhere between the nationalists and new Labour in an attempt to broaden its appeal. He sees the local appeal of the newspaper declining with the reduced number of local reporters. "The local papers are more geared up for that", whereas in the past there had been a local reporter for *The Western Mail* in Ammanford with "his finger on the pulse".
James Daniels, 31 August 2001

For the Protheroes the newspaper connects them with their past, providing continuity as their life has changed.

Geoff reads the legal notices as he used to when he worked at the bank and Angharad reads the births and deaths. "She always has", said Geoff.
Protheroe household, 15 September 2001

Other readers differ from Mr Daniels in that they feel that they have moved with the newspaper and in the process have constructed a new sense of their Welsh identity.

"The layout of *The Western Mail* is better now, it used to be a bit dour, it's easier to find the sections you're interested in, the new editor who took it over some years ago has really revamped it. The paper is completely different from when I first started reading it, but I'll always read it, it's an excellent paper."
Geoff Protheroe, 14 December 2001

Wales – more than other nations – is easily understood as a cultural construction, an imagined community.[73] It is imagined, however, in very different ways. Several of our respondents saw sport – specifically, rugby – as the event or occasion that unites Wales more than anything else. Paul Addey, discussing his idea of Wales and Welshness, expressed this forcefully.

> " … during rugby internationals the occasion transcends the game … the whole nation is us."
> Paul Addey, 10 May 2001

With the mass media, however, like most things except rugby, we find pan-Wales identification more problematic. Ieuan James, in north Wales, does not feel that Wales has a national newspaper. For him, television and radio broadcasting *in Welsh* has helped to create a sense of nation by partly overcoming the geographical divisions in Wales. Television has broadcast the differences between north and south and has exposed the north and south to one another, the different linguistic and cultural nuances. The James use the national (Welsh) media from time-to-time for coverage of special events – National Assembly for Wales elections, the National Eisteddfod, and national sporting events.

> *"Mae angen llawer mwy o bwnciau i wneud â'r gogledd ar y newyddion. Tydi newyddion lleol ddim yn cyrraedd y newyddion genedlaethol".* ["We need more north issues on Welsh news, there is a gap in terms of local news making it to the national stage."]
> Ieuan James, 30 May 2001

He sees a large and growing divide between north and south in terms of economy, politics and culture. He says that we have a better understanding of one another, in that we have "got used to each other", but that the press in Wales is still very parochial and fragmented.

Voicing a common concern about divisions within Wales, Ieuan saw national (Welsh) news as focused on south Wales with very little of local interest and very few local news stories for those in the north. Local news and information come from local newspapers – the regional *Daily Post* and the weekly *Caernarfon and Denbigh Herald, Bangor and Anglesey Mail, The Chronicle, Pioneer*, and *Llais Ogwan*. He felt that there is an unequal representation on the news at the national (Welsh) level, replicating the large and growing divide between north and south in economic, political and cultural terms. Ieuan agreed with his son that the BBC is London-biased, so not objective in its reporting.

73 Benedict Anderson (1983) *Imagined Communities: Reflections on the Origin and Spread of Nationalism*, London, Verso.

We examined uses of the Welsh-language television channel S4C. Generally, the numbers and the length of time spent watching Welsh-language output was surprisingly low, with none of our households including frequent viewers. Many watched the occasional programme, or watched some of the English language share of the channel's schedule (the Channel 4 programmes that are broadcast at different times on S4C). While most respondents liked the fact that Wales had its own television channel, we found strong and contradictory views about S4C, reflecting the diversity of Wales.

> *"Peidiwch a fy nghamddeall, mae'n holl bwysig i Gymru cael sianel Gymraeg. Mae hynny'n bwysig iawn ond 'dwi'n teimlo bod yna ormod o bwyslais a'r Gaerdydd a'r de. Mae'n trio'n rhy galed i fod yn trendi ac meant yn ein anghofio ni yn y gogledd".* ["Don't get me wrong, I think it's vital that Wales has its own channel. That's very important, but I get the feeling its very much Cardiff-based and southern-biased. It's trying too hard to be trendy and it's forgetting us here in the north."]
> *Ieuan James, 30 May 2001*

> "Every time I turn on S4C there's always some farmer from north Wales talking about sheep or something, it focuses too much on the north, besides to be honest, we need subtitles here in the south to understand them."
> *Brian Powell, 16 January 2002*

Dafydd Lewis expressed his feelings about the channel's appeal to the youth audience.

> "It comes across as trying too hard to be trendy and just looks false most of the time. On the whole it seems like it appeals more to my mother's age group and older."
> *Dafydd Lewis, 25 November 2001*

His mother puts across her views on how S4C has let its standard slip over recent years.

> "There's definitely too much bad language on S4C, it goes over the top sometimes in trying to attract a younger audience. I don't think it should go as low as some of the other channels. S4C should have a standard which it should not fall below … To be honest the quality of the programmes on S4C has fallen since I remember watching it regularly."

Our research subjects highlighted the problems facing S4C in trying to perform the functions of a national broadcaster and in contributing to the imagination of

Wales as a national community. As one channel, with limited scheduling time for Welsh-language output, S4C seems to have a difficult task in catering for the tastes of different generations, tastes and geography in a nation divided by its language.

Some of our research subjects made little or no association with Wales, and one expressed firmly negative views of Wales and its local and national media.

> It was clear that John found it difficult to relate in a positive manner to Welshness. For him, Merthyr is a "bad place to live" and he would be "out of here like a shot if I won the lottery". He and his work colleagues identify themselves as Welsh (possibly only through birth), but have very little interest in Welsh affairs or local news. He does not watch local or regional news, nor does he buy a local newspaper. He sees Wales as divided by the language and a north–south divide between those who think that they are the "true Welsh" (referring to those in the north) and the rest. "There are no Welsh-language road signs in Merthyr."
> *John Swaine, 15 May 2001*

As a premiership football fan, John was not drawn into the Welsh nation even by the rugby.

Another household, in Wrexham, identified closely with another region of the UK in that they opted out of Welsh broadcasting in favour of Granada and Channel 4 transmitted from England.

> "We get Channel 4 and Granada from Manchester. I don't have a clue what's going on in Wales sometimes, *The Daily Post* is quite good for that though. The Welsh news is all south Wales anyway. Granada is probably more relevant for us perhaps anyway. We all tend to go over the border for Christmas shopping and things. I mean we are so close to England, their news is our news really, I don't think we're missing out ... we have the BBC news and the ITV national news on, Granada news comes before the national news, so we watch it on occasion, well most nights actually, especially the late news, we never miss that ... I don't feel that it's not relevant to us, it's more relevant to us than the Welsh news, because that's all focused on the south. The Welsh-language channel is no good to us because we can't speak Welsh ... Granada really caters for us in this area I suppose. We don't watch the Welsh channel, not because we're anti the language, we've been to the Eisteddfod in Llangollen and really enjoyed it, it's just that Channel 4 is the same channel but without all the programmes

we can't understand, it's common sense for us to watch it. S4C is a channel for the Welsh speakers and that's a good thing I think, but I wouldn't watch it, in fact I can't imagine that many people watch it at all around here. However, it's a good status symbol for Wales, it puts us on the cultural map doesn't it? ... I suppose it does, but it costs us just the same, we're paying for something we never watch aren't we? ... It's good for Wales, but it's not really a channel that represents all the population ... It wouldn't be so bad if they had more English language programmes set in Wales. They would still be Welsh programmes – made in Wales, but we could all enjoy them. It wouldn't necessarily mean the language would die. At the end of the day, we are all Welsh, yet S4C don't really make us feel included in the vision it has, which is a shame."
Julie Riley, 6 November 2001

The Addey and Rowlands household – MTV viewers and computer games enthusiasts – are Welsh learners. They identify with new territories of transmission while maintaining a powerful commitment to the local, demonstrating forcefully how we are all, variously and unevenly, implicated in global integration.

Brian Powell reads *The Western Mail* every day, and is a good example of how various media are used to construct an orientation to local, national and global communities. In Brian's case, *The Western Mail* embodies his new sense of Welshness, represented by the affluent professional classes in south-east Wales. His use of the newspaper expresses his 'buying into' this new image of Wales.

"I like the business and sports sections as a rule. I glance at the headlines, they're always well laid-out so you get a good sense of what's happening here and abroad before the day starts ... you know, combine *The Western Mail* with the BBC *News*, especially on digital and there's all the news you need really. *The Western Mail* wouldn't really be enough for me otherwise, I need to know what's going on outside Wales as well in detail, but I think the coverage of Welsh political life is getting much better and the sport's always been top notch ... I get a lot of patients coming in, retired bank managers, headteachers and so on, it's good to keep up to date with a broad range of topics as a matter of course. I suppose I like to feel informed."
Brian Powell, 16 January 2002

Mr Daniels, too, mixes and matches his media, and is interested in both the very local (local history programmes on S4C) and the global (news, to keep up to date with the financial markets).

He regards *The Western Mail* as an essential read for entrepreneurs in Wales. "It's a must if you want to keep up with the future openings in business in Wales." He feels that the newspaper does not have the resources to compete with the London press for the big businessman who reads it for the financial news but "they do a good job, especially with their annual survey of the top 100 businesses in Wales". He sees the delivery of up-to-date information on Sky, Bloomberg and BBC News 24 as leaving the traditional print press behind. His consumption of broadcast political and financial news, he says, can be quantified as 80 per cent BBC News 24, 20 per cent Sky News.
James Daniels, 31 August 2001

We found one most extraordinary instance of mixing the local and global in the Daniels household.

> Mrs Daniels said that they have Sky digital, but there was a problem with the system and they could not get HTV Wales on the main set. Mr Daniels has got around this problem by having another full-size colour set in the living room. (The 'problem' was that, at this time, Sky did not broadcast ITV.) It was Sunday afternoon and BBC News 24 was on the main set. Mr Daniels switched on the other set after lunch to watch *Your Century*, a programme charting the local history of Wales. The programme was devoted to the Neath area from the early part of the twentieth century to the present day. Mr Daniels watched this programme on the television on the left side of the room, while BBC News 24 on Sky remained on throughout on the other set. Occasionally he would turn the sound down on HTV to pay attention to a particular news story on the news channel. He switched between the two programmes on several occasions, with the sounds of the two programmes occasionally competing with one another. Mr Daniels seemed happy with both sets satisfying his selective form of attention, admittedly to the amazement of the rest of the household.

> Mrs Daniels said, "It's amazing, why we don't just phone the company to put it right I don't know. Have you ever seen anything like it, two televisions on in the living room at the same time, with the chief sitting in the middle? [laughing at this point] … He's off now to phone his friend to tell him to watch the programme on HTV, he's not right."
> *Elizabeth Daniels, 23 September 2001*

Mr Daniels thus shows one particular way in which the local and global are mutually compatible. In another household Mark James and his father discussed their feelings about the significance of global networks for people in Wales. They commented on how they saw the future of Welsh identity in the face of global influence and contacts in cyberspace.

> Mark said, "Fydd bod yn Gymraeg yn bwysicach efo cyberspace", ["being Welsh will become more important with cyberspace",] and his Dad adds that "*fydd o ddim mor syml a hynny … heb ofal a gweithio ati, gallwn golli ein hunaniaeth*". ["it won't be quite that simple … without care and having to work at it, our identity could be lost".] If we do not work at keeping the language, he continues, then it will be lost on the global stage, and if we rely on the Web for our experiences of each other then we might well lose the skills of face-to-face interaction and, in Wales, the skills of our indigenous language. The loss of language skills, they agreed, meant the loss of identity.
> *Ieuan and Mark James, 14 May 2001*

For the Protheroes, digital technology is an important means of maintaining links with Wales when at their second home in France. They demonstrate how, in a context in which dozens of channels are available, a sense of identity linked to geographical place (Wales) remains vitally important. Satellite technology allows local television channels and radio stations (in this case from Wales) to be received abroad, and thus enhances their local identification while they are abroad.[74]

> "We subscribe to Sky here and Canal Plus in France. We have it because we want to have British television when we're abroad for a long period … especially BBC Wales and Radio Wales. It's important that we still have the news from home, because we're probably away for five months of the year and we rent the house for the rest of the time … I just insert the Sky card into the Sky decoder out there and we can get most of the same channels, but we pay extra to Canal Plus for using the service, that's on top of our subscription to them. It is quite expensive I think, but it's worth it to have a link back home. I think we just pay for the unlocking of the extra Sky channels, their satellite picks it up and our card and decoder unscramble it … Really, it's mainly for things like the news, the BBC news, for political and financial news."

---

74 This exemplifies Anthony Giddens' argument that social relationships are increasingly 'lifted out' of situated locales and disembedded – stretched across sometimes vast geographical distances. See A. Giddens (1990) *The Consequences of Modernity*, Cambridge, Polity.

Angharad said, "The Welsh news makes us feel at home ... I suppose it's easier to look at all the gloom back home, when you're in the heart of France, things don't seem as bad there, you're distanced from the news of unemployment and crime and things like that back home ... Yes it's the news mainly and sometimes the sport, I've been known to watch the Six Nations from France ... you can get English papers out there, but really not any Welsh papers, so the BBC Wales news is all the news we get from back home, I mean we need to know what's happening because we live in Wales for the majority of the year, you can't cut the cord really."
Protheroe household, 26 January 2002

This might be seen as a modern variant of having had *The Western Mail* sent to them in London.

The Swaines, in contrast to the Protheroes, have effectively removed themselves from Wales. The Swaines appreciate Sky enormously but have no need for local broadcasting. Sky meets all their needs.

"I'm not really interested in local sport, I never watch the local news, there's nothing on the normal channels. I'd go mad if I didn't have Sky, there's just nothing to watch before I go to work and when I come home."
John Swaine, 23 October 2001

Other households are less polarised – they successfully mix the local with the global. The Rileys, as we discussed, regularly email pictures of themselves to their daughter in Canada.

We reported in Chapter 3 how Dafydd Lewis generally preferred *Loaded* to S4C. He uses the media to express and sustain his identification with Ibiza clubbing culture, whereas his mother uses the local and regional press to reinforce her identification with the local, with Builth Wells and Wales. In this case there is a clear generational aspect to spaces of identity. The older people in our research tended to use the media more to identify with their locality and with Wales. Having said that, Addey and Rowlands in Swansea are in their twenties and have a very strong sense of local commitment – albeit while consuming their diet of MTV and PS2.

With greater global connection we found that the imagined other and the global are now accessed more easily and more extensively from home. Foreign stations, however, were mistrusted, or seen as less authoritative, by many.

"We've started to try and watch the news a lot more since the terrorist attacks and the Afghanistan thing has kicked off ... the news channels seem

to report it differently. You have to be sceptical about the way they report, because you don't know whose interest they represent. I distrust the news anyway. I'll watch BBC News 24 if I'm bored, it's better than the American news channels. I mean look at ABC news in America, they're partly owned by Disney, or is it CNN, one of them anyway. You don't see them reporting on sweatshops making Mickey Mouse dolls do you, or on the fact that McDonalds fund the IRA."
Christopher Rowlands, 15 October 2001

I asked them about the news and how they felt events were reported. Karen thinks that "the BBC are about the best, they don't sensationalise, they just report what's going on. Some of the American news stations seem to make up the news a bit more, but I trust the BBC." Dafydd said, "I'll watch the news to find out what's going on in the world, I don't trust the pictures I see coming from the Arab stations about the war. I think in this country we try and get the real picture a bit more. I'll sit and watch the news, I suppose, because it's important to know what's going on."
Karen and Dafydd Lewis, 25 October 2001

Whatever the processes of globalisation, we found complex senses of identity, tied to language and place – albeit with national culture meaning very different things to different people. There can be no doubt that a multiplicity of channels and technologies reduces the capacity of the major broadcasting institutions to speak to and construct the nation. Such cultural apparatuses do not simply reflect or express the nation, they produce it; so new communication practices, such as multi-channel television, change how national identity is constructed.[75] It seems that *The Western Mail* has managed to hold its traditional core while feminising and modernising, representing and constructing a new Wales.[76]

Unsurprisingly, we found that in their consumption of local, national and global media, individuals work with clear connections between their locality and their identity. We found a continuing resilience of the local in the context of globalisation,[77] including a strong identification with some sense of the Welsh nation (disenchanted, patriotic, elitist or otherwise). Thus the tensions between the

---

75   Philip Schlesinger (1991) *Media, State and Nation: Political Violence and Collective Identities*, London, Sage.

76   At the time of our research *The Western Mail* could be described as a Welsh quality and an essential 'second buy' for the business and professional elite in Wales. Subsequently, under a new editor, it has positioned itself as something more akin to *The Daily Mail*.

77   Sales of weekly newspapers in the UK are holding up, while those of daily and Sunday nationals are falling.

local, national and global are resolved in our households. Rather than worrying about the negative effects of global media, the issue we identified was the diversity of the population of Wales. This offers a challenge to the media – especially those that are committed to constructing a sense of Welshness that goes beyond the feeling of identification that is engendered on specific occasions, notably international rugby matches.

The Welsh language

This section explores some issues about the Welsh language and the media in Wales, an issue of considerable significance because of the centrality of the language (as opposed to institutions, for example) to national identity in Wales.[78] We examine uses of the media by speakers and learners of the language and we consider some of the linguistic divisions in Wales. We found Welsh speakers expressing cultural elitism and non-Welsh speakers articulating stereotypes of Welsh speakers – with important implications for Welsh media that are concerned to reach a pan-Wales market. Cultural factors mean that bridging the linguistic divide in Wales remains problematic.

Welsh speakers and English monoglots in our households seemed to fall into two distinct groups. Welsh speakers were all in business or professional occupations whereas our working class households were all English-only speakers – unlike the traditional association of the Welsh language with the *gwerin*, the common folk. Unfortunately our two Welsh-speaking households were Welsh-speaking only in terms of capability, not practice – so in none of our households was Welsh the main everyday language of the home, although in a number of households it was used frequently by some household members. To be fair to the Welsh-language media, this is a caveat that needs to be stressed. Unfortunately, in a project of the duration of this one, we had no time to remedy this deficiency in our sample. That we found households able to speak Welsh fluently but not doing so in practice points to the issue of the use of the language at home by those able to speak it and the complexity of language use.[79]

We found two Welsh learners, both in the same household, and explored how they found breaking into the language (for the first time since school). We

78   For a summary of issues about the Welsh language today see John Aitchison and Harold Carter (2000) *Language, Economy and Society. The Changing Fortunes of the Welsh Language in the Twentieth Century*, Cardiff, University of Wales Press.

79   For example, only just over half of Welsh speaking households are wholly Welsh speaking, and in south Wales under a third of Welsh speakers use Welsh most or all of the time. See Colin Williams (ed) (2000) *Language Revitalization Policy and Planning in Wales*, Cardiff, University of Wales Press.

followed their use of S4C programming and subtitles (on teletext 888) as their learning developed.

> "We watch a lot of S4C and S4C Digital because we're trying to learn Welsh as well, so it's on a lot so we can hear the language even when you're not watching it, you can hear the language and pick up on words. So maybe if you can't speak it, you can start understanding little bits and bobs of what's going on, it's nice to have it on ... I find because I've got more Welsh-speaking friends now, they help me along, even if it's just making me say colours, or directions like left and right when we're in the car. It all helps, I still watch S4C, but mostly in the background, I'll pick up certain words especially if it's a music show or something, you know, something you can relate to. I tend to listen to things like Radio Cymru in the car with my mate, mostly 'cos he's done some music for it and he speaks Welsh, so I get a fair bit of exposure to it I suppose."
> *Christopher Rowlands, 17 June 2001*

Paul Addey does not watch S4C on a regular basis, but watches the occasional programme on S4C to help his learning, though he finds programmes without 888 subtitles too hard to follow. With programmes where there is a mix of Welsh and English he can at least follow the plot.

> "I used to watch the kids' shows on *Planed Plant*, but I've lost interest really, it's better if you've got Welsh speakers around you, isn't it? ... If you watch the rugby or something, it's in a context you can understand. I just don't get to speak it much in real life and when I do it's spoken really fast and it leaves me behind a bit. I notice that Welsh is spoken very quickly, compared to say English. I watch a lot of like the children's TV, you know, because, you know, it's like the Welsh equivalent of *Sesame Street*, so I'm starting to learn things like going round the clock. They're teaching you how to tell the time, they're teaching Welsh-speaking kids, but it's basic enough for me to kind of grasp it. Maybe stuff like a Welsh music programme, because loads of young people are into things like *Jools Holland Show*, and *Pop Factory* on BBC2, but if they had that kind of thing in Welsh. It's like the Welsh coverage of the rugby, because you're interested in it, you tend to pick up the language as well. Like on S4C Digital they've got *Pobol y Cwm* with subtitles, that's a great idea."
> *Paul Addey, 17 June 2001*

In households with no Welsh-speaking members we explored views of the

Welsh-language media and, more generally, Welsh speakers. The usual pejorative stereotypes were expressed, but some also said that to be Welsh one must speak the language.

> Paul thought that S4C gave a "look over the fence" at a different kind of Welsh culture. When pushed on this point, he said that he felt that he could see that there was a Welsh culture on display that he did not feel a part of and that learning the language would in some way open this up for him. I asked Paul if he thought he would feel 'more' Welsh if he could speak the language. He said that he feels "semi-Welsh" and does not feel a part of the same Welshness as seen on S4C. Paul feels outside Welsh culture as this is represented on S4C but says that elitism is too harsh a word to describe how he sees it.
> *Paul Addey, 10 May 2001*

Others show how individual attitudes and stereotypes remain obstacles for Welsh-language broadcasting.

> Nicola told me that, of course, she is Welsh. However, she saw those who went to Welsh schools as snobs when she was younger. She tells me that she feels bad about this now and would love to learn the language: she should, to be really Welsh, or "proper Welsh". She has no interest in Welsh-language broadcasting, and does not think that there is anything of interest on it for her. She never watches Welsh-language output on S4C. She hopes that Louise will pick it up and sometimes has *Planed Plant* [*Children's Planet*] on at her mum's to help her along, but not often.

> "Well I don't watch Welsh programmes because I don't understand them, I wouldn't watch them with subtitles either ... I don't know why, I suppose there's not really anything on there that would make me watch it with the subtitles on. I watch S4C if there's something like *Friends* or a film, you know if I'm flicking through the channels to see what's on ... I am Welsh, I feel Welsh even though I don't speak the language. Cardiff's a pretty mixed place now, it's not really about the language is it, these days? ... There's a lot of people in Wales who don't speak Welsh and speak a whole range of languages, so I mean, to say being Welsh is about speaking the language is a bit sad."
> *Nicola Davies, 14 January 2002*

The Swaines believe that Sky caters for all their needs. They did not even know whether they received S4C or not. When we asked, Michelle Swaine flicked through the multitude of digital channels to find out.

"There's enough choice now so we don't watch it [S4C] ... things on there are all Welsh." Michelle said that she feels that she should speak Welsh, but the programmes have no interest for her. Her husband, however, does not even consider himself Welsh as his father was Irish. She says that he hates Wales (although he was born in Wales) because there is nothing for the children and no employment prospects.
Michelle Swaine, 23 May 2001

John Swaine said that he has never watched S4C and very rarely watches BBC Wales or HTV anymore – since they got Sky. He never watches the news and does not read any local or Welsh newspapers. He does not "see the point in Welsh-language output because I've never met anyone who speaks Welsh", not many people have an interest in the Welsh language and so Welsh-language programming is pointless and irrelevant.
John Swaine, 23 May 2001

On the other side we heard the voice of the first-language Welsh speaker. Mr Daniels, too, hints at a sense of true Welshness and something else that is second class.

Mr Daniels was keen to examine my roots in Wales, commenting that "people from Swansea aren't really Welsh are they?" He sees the future of the language as dependent on Welsh communities thriving and the language being passed down the generations through use in the household. "Well, you either speak the language or you don't. I don't see the point of watching it on the television if you're going to go out and speak English in work or in the street."
James Daniels, 14 July 2001

In the case of Stuart Chandler and Ann Thomas we saw the linguistic dilemma and its implications for their Welsh identity from the position of individuals with limited Welsh language ability. Both understand and can speak some Welsh but are not fluent enough for conversation. In the course of their work they frequently come into contact with the Welsh-speaking farming community in Wales on the telephone.

Stuart described how farmers call in Welsh and he has to speak in English: "Sorry, I don't speak Welsh." "Oh, English are you?" Stuart feels annoyed by this and states that being neither English nor a Welsh speaker makes

him feel like a kind of "mongrel race". His employers like the workforce to speak Welsh but do not actively encourage them to learn during office time.
Stuart Chandler, 22 May 2001

In another of our households the media seem to have enhanced the ability to speak and learn Welsh.

The Lewis boys attend the local comprehensive (in a predominately English-speaking area), but are taught through the medium of Welsh, in 'Welsh units'. They are separated from most of the other pupils into smaller classes for most subjects. The boys describe this as causing an "us and them" mentality among the pupils. This has improved over the years, but has in the past led to feelings of being an "outcast". The boys feel that the class sizes in the Welsh medium classes are an advantage to their education, but that they are at a disadvantage when it comes to revision, because there are more textbooks and revision aids in English and a shortfall of Welsh-language publications. They tell me that they used to be called "Welshies", but this has got better since programmes like *Pam fi, Duw?*, *Sgorio* and *Y Clwb Rygbi* have been on S4C, because their friends now have an interest in learning the language, to be able to enjoy these programmes. The boys are popular because they can translate the commentary. They would like to see more Welsh speakers in the area. Karen feels that they sometimes stick out and that there is a divide between the linguistic groups in the area. Karen and the boys feel that Welsh will help them to "get on" in terms of future job prospects. They feel that the language has a much better status these days. Dafydd wants to go to a Welsh university to study because he wants to keep and improve his Welsh and to stay close to home.
Karen Lewis, 6 September 2001

Associating the language with upward social mobility was something we found in other households.

The household is Welsh-speaking, although its members converse with one another in English almost all of the time. Gareth goes to a Welsh-medium school and Brian and Rhian are both from industrial south Wales. The children's Welsh fluency is significantly greater than that of their parents. Although their parents have conversational Welsh passed down from their parents, the children have a greater ability in the written language. Rhian and Brian speak to their parents in Welsh and can understand Welsh-language programmes on S4C. They reported that their language skills

deteriorated after childhood: they had no Welsh-speaking friends at college nor, until very recently, any Welsh-speaking neighbours. Both Rhian and Brian value the language as a mean of "getting on" in Wales.
Brian Powell, 1 November 2001

While in Mr James we found an approach to the Welsh language that borders on elitism, we also found Welsh speakers who felt that their perspectives were absent from the mass media. The James family commented on a recent political row about the Welsh language.

We discussed the race row that has been generated by the comments made by Beca Brown in the Welsh magazine *Barn*. There have been several news stories reporting local officials and Plaid Cymru councillors in north Wales. Ieuan said that he felt that it was unfair that their comments had been taken out of context by the media. "Things can be said and done against the Welsh, but it is not acceptable to say anything against the English", he said, and referred to Anne Robinson's pejorative comments about the Welsh. He said that the media had reported what was essentially a Welsh language and cultural issue as a racist issue. For him it is not an issue of race but socio-economics – Welsh people are priced out of the local housing market, people who might in the first instance be forced to move away to find employment, leaving property for sale in the area. He regards the influx of English migrants as of secondary concern to that of Welsh-speaking youngsters being forced to move away to gain work. "The news has not facilitated intelligent debate, by making it a racist issue, people tend to shy away from racist debate but it is a legitimate debate in Wales … Beca Brown's comments were taken out of context and others have had a knee-jerk reaction to this. The media have turned a legitimate debate into sensationalist headlines."
Ieuan James, 29 August 2001

With the significant caveat that, unfortunately, our two Welsh-speaking households did not use their Welsh in their everyday life at home, we found little use of Welsh-language media. Among those who watched S4C, generally, the numbers watching and the amount of time spent watching Welsh-language output was low, with none of our households claiming to contain frequent viewers. Many watched the occasional programme, and most watched some of the English language share of the channel's schedule.

The Powells do not read the Welsh-language columns of *The Western Mail*. Rhian watches *Pobol y Cwm* on S4C, without the subtitles – but other than this uses

S4C only for *Brookside*, *Countdown* and *Fifteen to One* (on the odd occasion when she comes home early). Brian watches sport in Welsh – he finds the language of the commentary at about his level. Their son, Gareth, does not watch much Welsh-language television.

> "I do watch it sometimes, if my friends at school are watching and they start talking about it. I'll watch it if it's supposed to be good. I was watching *Fondue, Rhyw a Deinosors* and I used to watch *Pam fi, Duw?* which was popular at school a while back. I usually watch *Sgorio* and *Y Clwb Rygbi*. Me and dad usually watch the rugby on S4C; they always show the better games and the internationals."
> *Gareth Powell, 1 November 2001*

Rather like Gareth, Dafydd Lewis sees S4C programmes as "too old-fashioned on the whole", with not much appeal for 17 year olds.

Angharad Protheroe reads Hafina Clwyd's Welsh-language column in *The Western Mail*. She does not always agree with her and finds her quite outspoken, but they are the same age and she finds it an interesting read on Thursdays. Sometimes she watches the 7 o'clock news on S4C. She says that she understands only about 80 per cent of what is said, finding the Welsh "too northern".

We discussed the Welsh-only nature of S4C productions with our research subjects. One of our Welsh learners was among several who thought that the status quo was the correct position.

> "I still think S4C do more than enough to cater for English speakers, it's like the people who move to Wales and complain that their children have to learn Welsh, its ridiculous. You don't come to a country, not do any groundwork about the culture, you wouldn't move to France or Spain, and not realise that your kids will have to learn French or Spanish in school. I don't think we need to water down S4C any more, if people want to watch it they should make some effort to learn the language. Why shouldn't we speak Welsh in Wales."
> *Christopher Rowlands, 15 October 2001*

Some people want to learn the Welsh language and feel that they will gain some intrinsic rewards if they do so. We heard that the language is the foundation of Welsh identity – and also that it is completely irrelevant in contemporary Wales. Some non-Welsh speakers, and certainly our Welsh learners, expressed an intrinsic need to be able to speak the language, or even guilt at not being able to do so. Not speaking the language was seen as the missing piece of the puzzle –

which has positive and negative implications for the media. Positively, there is a sense that the media and broadcasting in particular can bridge this gap. Negatively, however, this sense of identity linked to language also means polarisation and disenfranchisement from the Welsh-language media.

In a sense there is a wall dividing the population of Wales. Some take a peek over the wall, but most find it hard to break through and step into the garden. Others on both sides build the wall even higher, which is a problem for the future of the language and for the media. As well as a huge divide between Welsh speakers and non-Welsh speakers, the Welsh-speaking community we found was far from homogenous, with those in the north seeing the Welsh media as south-centric.

Some felt that to ensure the lasting and broad appeal of Welsh-language broadcasting, there must be a move away from essentialist constructs of Welsh identity tied to the language. We found several bilingual households within which language is mixed in a way that is natural to their members. In such households the media consumed, however, is weighted very heavily towards English-language output — perhaps because of a lack of bilingual broadcasting stations or channels in Wales.

Our many households with mixed language ability and with learners provide a model of bilingualism that could inform the media in Wales. We identified a general desire for a more inclusive media in Wales, an umbrella for the cultural and linguistic diversity that is found in Wales, and a feeling that the current offerings did not meet expectations on this count.

Chapter 5

Conclusions

Our research has mapped some of the diversity of contemporary media consumption practices in Wales. We have charted some of the richness of media use, and examined how media users engage with their various media in their homes, and how these media are interleaved – with both one another and with other activities. Engagement with the media follows a great variety of styles, but in ways that are patterned. Media consumption is shaped by everyday life, which is constrained or patterned by a range of broader cultural features. This is a far from a one-way process, in that at the same time the media exercise their own constraints and patternings on everyday life in the domestic sphere.

Decisions about newspaper delivery were likely to be made by men, who tend to read the newspaper first and to prefer national and international news. Men read more in the living room, women more in the kitchen. Women prefer local news, and were the main buyers of local newspapers. Local newspapers are sometimes bought for specific reasons, such as television guides, local sport and employment. Obviously, they are commonly read for local news and events, but they are usually not read in any depth but used on a 'pick and flick' basis. National newspapers are appreciated for their broader coverage, especially of current affairs, but also for their lifestyle supplements. Styles of reading newspapers relate to gender, age and lifestyle, with the level of engagement with the newspaper depending in large part on the amount of time available. Men and women like different sections and different lifestyle supplements. Newspapers are used for relaxation and as withdrawal from other people and activity, to create personal space. For some, especially younger adults, periodicals are more important than newspapers. They are selected because they reflect buyers' lifestyles, and are used in similar ways and for similar purposes as newspapers.

Radio's strength is its undemanding nature, which means that it can be combined with another activity – but this also means that, being largely background, its significance is low-key and general. It is used mainly in the kitchen, notably during the kitchen routines of breakfast and washing-up, and also when cleaning. It is appreciated as background, for the mediated company that it provides, and as a means to fill household space with sound. At the least active end of the listening spectrum it is hardly listened to at all. At the most active end, a particular programme or presenter is listened to attentively – but this is rare. Between are degrees of background versus attentive listening. Radio is often used to create an ambience, or soundscape, to accompany some other activity. Music television challenges the radio, in that it is used in some households for the same sorts of purposes. At the same time, radio by cable or satellite extends the appeal of radio, making stations more accessible (by use of the remote control) and moving radio into the living room (making it a background medium in *leisure* space).

We found a diversity of expectations regarding television use, from an almost religious commitment to particular soaps or sports programmes to more wide-spread and mundane uses. Much television viewing is undertaken with low expectations. While particular programmes are very important to some people, much of the remainder is 'filler' or 'wallpaper', providing the background for some other activity, notably relaxation. In all households new television forms (for example, 'reality' television) are challenging the categories of 'drama' and 'documentary', and changing how viewers identify with the programmes. In multi-channel households we identified new styles of television viewing: 24-hour news and video-on-demand provide a new way of conceiving of broadcasting, empowering the consumer in terms of their control of time. In some multi-channel households this was accompanied not just by more varied viewing patterns, but also by less use of the video shop and the VCR. An extreme variant of the new style of television viewing was the growth of channel-flicking, facilitated by EPGs. With an on-screen display of alternative possibilities, viewers are distracted from engaging with a broadcast by technology that foregrounds the alternative possibilities. Individuals like to get their programme information from a number of sources. The most popular of these, and all that is available in terrestrial households, is the television listings in newspapers and magazines. Local newspapers, in particular, were commonly reported to be bought mainly for the television listings and reviews. EPGs were used more for synchronic programme selection than for planning future viewing.

Like other media, new media serve both to bring people together and to construct personal space. We found a vibrant gaming culture among younger males. This was highly interactive and social, and a part of a lively subculture. Games consoles have won a place in the living room – the preferred location in those households that had more than one games player. In these, gaming is a highly social, collective activity. We found that PCs in the home were used surprisingly little. Their major use was to work more flexibly (in spatial and temporal terms), transforming the boundary between home and work. They are also used for research (to inform consumer decisions) and to keep in contact (by email). The use of email was widespread and popular in Internet households. Most usage is pragmatic and time spent on the Internet is relatively short – because of cost, some reported. There were concerns about security and viruses, but a growing acceptability of Internet shopping, particularly with already-known high-street names. Some reported that the novelty of the Internet had worn off, though many recognised its utility. PCs were located away from the living space, and were engaged with as a solitary activity – albeit one that engages with distant or virtual others. We found teletext to be ignored in most households, though appreciated for the 888 service in households with Welsh learners.

Media use in households is shaped by, and in turn shapes, the temporal patterning of household life. The media are used to structure time, to pass time and to make time (for oneself). Time in households is shaped profoundly by generation, or stage in the lifecycle. Men are more able to make time for their media consumption. VCRs, multi-channel television and 24 hour news disrupt the flow of television and the power of broadcasters and their schedules, and lead to a very different style of engagement with television.

In many households the living room is where members of the household come together. In others the living room is dominated by males. We found fragmentation in media use, to create personal time and space, mostly in bedrooms (for children) but also in the kitchen (for women). With multiple sets, VCRs and other entertainment devices in bedrooms and the kitchen, more privatised forms of consumption are facilitated. Multi-channel television, however, operates to bring people together again in the living room, around the new family hearth, with wide-screen television and multimedia entertainment systems. This challenges the recent trend towards the growing privatisation of media consumption. Uses of different spaces by men and women, and by younger and older members of households, connect with different styles of viewing, listening and reading.

The politics of the domestic sphere, power in the home, is crucial for understanding how the media are consumed – and gender is one key dimension of this. We found women acting as moral guardians for their household in relation to media consumption, voicing fears about quality and quantity and deprecating the widespread or unregulated consumption of television. They and their families generally watched more television than they suggested at the outset. We found men the main choosers of what newspapers are bought and delivered, and clear differences between not just which newspapers, but which sections of newspapers, are read by men and women. We found women to be more interested in local news and soaps, and men to be more interested in national and international newspapers and news programmes. New media technologies – multi-channel television, the Internet, EPGs and computer games – were generally bought, installed and operated by men. The arrangements connecting the television to the hi-fi and other apparatuses in the living room mystified many women. Women felt excluded from these new technologies, found them incomprehensible and saw them as 'male gadgets'. Most women in our study could not operate the VCR to record or, in multi-channel households, use the EPG. So EPGs remained unused by some household members, especially women, and many interactive services were avoided because they were not understood or did not work. Clearly, many aspects and features of digital, while technically possible and available on the market, have a long way to go to win time and space in the home. In households with multi-channel television, local newspapers and television listings guides were used mostly by women – who preferred them to EPGs. Several women felt uncomfortable about the technologisation of their living rooms and hung on to more traditional media (radio, local newspapers and terrestrial television) and the kitchen for their regular media use.

Place and history, or biography, are clearly very important – obviously for senses of identity, but also for patterns of media consumption. We have seen how biography or identity connects with sometimes very strong views on components of the Welsh media landscape. This shows not just how media consumption is contingent and situated, but how this is a long-standing matter, and unlikely to be something that can be transformed quickly or easily. We found strong support for *The Western Mail*, rooted firmly in senses of Wales and Welshness. For readers of *The Western Mail* the newspaper has been for a long period of time, and remains, very important for constructing and sustaining their sense of nation and national identity. The paper was supported despite or because of its feminisation and modernisation. Some of its readers feel that they have moved with the newspaper in constructing a new (south-east Wales) sense of Welsh identity. Broadcasting is seen by many as having connected north and south Wales, but the notion of 'Welsh news' is hardly recognised in the north. There are many ways in which people in Wales connect with the nation and its language, with strong feelings on all sides. Several saw sport – specifically, rugby – as the event or occasion that unites Wales more than anything else. In most households a strong sense of local identification co-existed happily with increasing uses of global media. Local newspapers continue as an important but relatively minor medium, the main source of local news. News broadcasts by television involved a varying balance of the local, Welsh, UK and global, and we identified a strong demand for more English-language Welsh programming. Whatever the processes of globalisation, in Wales we found complex senses of identity, tied to place and in many cases connected to language – with national culture meaning very different things to different people. The temporal flexibility and choice of programming offered by multi-channel television were strongly appreciated by subscribing households, which clearly transforms but does not remove an interest in the local and a demand for Welsh media.

It is unfortunate that, while two of our households contained members that were all fluent Welsh-speakers, these were not Welsh-speaking households in the sense that they lived their everyday domestic lives in Welsh. Noting this important caveat, we found very little use of Welsh-language media in these households or in our three mixed-language households and one learner household. S4C and 888 subtitles were appreciated by the Welsh learners. The language was tolerated by most non-Welsh speakers, rejected entirely by one, and seen as the heart of Welsh culture by others. We found a great diversity of perspectives on the Welsh language, including elitist notions of cultural purity and a total rejection of any place for the language in Wales today. We found major differences between Welsh speakers in the north and south, as well as between Welsh speakers and English monoglots, and between non-speakers, learners and speakers of Welsh. Mixed-language households may provide some interesting lessons for the media in seeking to address a pan-Wales market.

Each household shows very different patterns of media use, demonstrating the enormous diversity of households and cultures that are to be found in one small country today. Although the environment will have already changed, we have provided a snapshot of some of the complexity and dynamics of media use in the contemporary era.

APPENDIX: RESEARCH METHODS

The method of this research is ethnography – involving extended fieldwork, a focus on insiders' meanings, and a way of handling data and writing up. This is a claim not made lightly because (as others have pointed out)[80] 'ethnography' is a term that has been used by media researchers in a cavalier way – to refer to very brief periods of observation, in-depth interviews or merely a commitment to identifying actors' meanings and understandings. It is a very narrow version of ethnography that has been imported to the study of the media – not a whole way of life, but a single medium or even genre[81] – hence one researcher has referred to it as 'an abused buzzword in our field'.[82] At the same time, for media organisations, it has become something of a holy grail, offering as it does the possibility of exploring in greater richness the growing diversity of consumption practices and complementing or challenging quantitative data and reported accounts of media consumption.

At the outset, the media organisations involved with the project specified their requirements regarding the number of households we studied and their characteristics. This was finally agreed as follows:

- At least four *The Western Mail* readers
- At least four Radio Wales listeners
- At least two Radio Cymru listeners
- All will receive Welsh broadcasting
- At least three S4C Welsh-language programming viewing households
- At least five Welsh-speaking households, probably three fully Welsh-speaking and two with some members Welsh-speaking and others not
- At least one household pre-, during and post- the child-caring stage of the lifecycle.
- A three-generational household

80 Marie Gillespie (1995) *Television, Ethnicity and Cultural Change*, London, Routledge.

81 Janice Radway (1988) 'Reception study: ethnography and the problems of dispersed audiences and nomadic subjects', *Cultural Studies*, vol. 2, no. 3, pp. 359–376.

82 James Lull (1990) *Inside Family Viewing: Ethnographic Research on Television's Audiences*, London, Routledge, p. 242.

- A mix of socio-economic classes

- Households with different working patterns (unemployed, two working adults, one working, and so on)

- At least one rural household

- Two households with cable or satellite

- One household with digital

- One or two households with Internet access, ideally one where it is 'always on'

- One household with a keen computer games (on TV screen) player

- Hopefully a *Daily Post* reader

Details of each household are provided in Chapter 3 – which shows that this, perhaps rather demanding, set of criteria was met in full, except that one household received English not Welsh broadcasting and we had no three-generational family.

Two of our households (Powell and Protheroe) were composed of fluent Welsh speakers, but unfortunately it transpired that members of these households did not use Welsh in their everyday lives. We have, however, gathered considerable data on media consumption in households where *some* Welsh is spoken. In two households Welsh was the predominant language, spoken by all bar the mother (Daniels and James). One household spoke Welsh regularly but not as the main language (Lewis). One household was composed of two Welsh learners (Addey and Rowlands), and in another a little Welsh was understood but they could not hold a conversation in Welsh (Chandler and Thomas). Thus the research spans households with a range of Welsh-speaking capacities, but unfortunately it did not include a household where *all* members of the household routinely speak Welsh to one another.

After an average of six hours fieldwork in each of the six households we wrote an Interim Report. This was discussed by the Project Steering Group, which decided that we would 'drop' two of our six households and recruit a further six – in order to meet the sampling criteria that had been established at the outset. For the purposes of this book we have not drawn on the two households that were dropped in this way.

We make no claims of typicality or generalisability – as is usually the case with ethnographic research. But, while researching ten households was ambitious and not easy, we have gathered detailed data on what – for research of this kind – is a fairly large number of households.

It was decided that a form of pragmatic sampling was the best strategy – contacting 'friends of friends'. In other words, the researcher asked friends to find suitable people, who he himself had not met – with the intermediary offering some vouchsafe for each party. This allowed some reassurance, or personal recommendation, but allowed the maintenance of greater distance than would be possible if the researcher already knew the research subjects. Such a strategy was not easy – especially to meet the sampling requirements within the available time-span. Generally, however, it has been a remarkably successful approach. It has been greatly facilitated by the standing of The Open University, which has tended to open doors.

At the outset our research subjects were contacted with a short telephone call, in which the aims of the project were discussed, but without revealing the extent of the commitment that would be required on their part. We emphasised the value of the research and the importance of the contribution that they would be able to make. The main purpose of this telephone call was to arrange an initial meeting, at which the project could be discussed further. Initial responses were varied, ranging from suspicion, through compliance, to enthusiasm and pleasure at having an opportunity to be associated with research at The Open University or about the Welsh media. Making arrangements was time-consuming and often disappointing. Holidays and other times when people were not available were a serious logistical problem. There were five rejections at the stage of these telephone calls.

The next part of the strategy was to develop a relationship with each household's members. How this was done varied between households, but in all cases an initial visit was followed by a request for completion of a diary, recording one week's media consumption, by each member of the household. The diaries proved useful as a rationale for arranging a subsequent visit to collect and discuss them. At the same time they restricted the development of an observation role, in that they were seen by several informants as embodying the research, as constituting the heart of the data-gathering. This meant the need to re-start, or renegotiate, a relationship that would lead to fieldwork. To avoid this problem, with the households where we began fieldwork later, the commitment expected – 30 hours fieldwork was our target – was made clear at the outset.

At all stages, and to progress from visitor to participant observer, success depended on being accepted. In one household the family pet seemed to perform the role of critical gatekeeper: the whole family stopped and waited while the dog checked out the researcher, his acceptance was received with relief, and a cup of tea followed. In other households, being accepted by the children seemed crucial; one parent was quite explicit that this was necessary. Developing common ground, perhaps on the basis of mutual interests or activities, was an important way of generating acceptability and relationships. From one household our researcher borrowed a martial arts video, with another he watched a cycle race at the weekend, and with a third he found himself cleaning out the gutters.

To varying degrees, more relaxed contact developed and richer data were gathered. This progress was dependent on being seen as acceptable, generating trust, and on the researcher's presence becoming seen as more natural and less of an intrusion.

Semi-structured interviews – with open-ended, non-directive questioning – were undertaken with all household members on several occasions. This allowed us to explore topics in which we were interested and matters we had observed. It allowed some element of triangulation, checking the validity of what had been said or done. It was also a way of exploring the significance of media use through discussion, particularly in more elusive areas, especially those relating to understanding the inherently private nature of much media use.

At the heart of the research, however, was extended fieldwork: an average of 26 hours per household, in each of the ten households, between May 2001 and February 2002. This involved observing and participating in a breadth of household activities, including media consumption. Initially, fieldwork in different households was inter-leaved. Later it became more 'blocked', in other words, a contiguous period of time was spent in a household. Towards the very end some unarranged visits were made, demonstrating the high level of access that had become available.

Notes were made – sometimes during, and sometimes immediately after, this fieldwork. These recorded as much detail as possible, with speech recorded as near to verbatim as possible. We drew maps of the settings, made recordings using audio and video recorders and took photographs. Recordings were transcribed, and these and other fieldnotes were discussed regularly by the two researchers. Second-tier notes – reflections on the fieldwork – were made by both researchers as the research progressed.

We do not see our work as naturalism in any sense – as presenting some account of the world as it is. There is no such thing as a neutral or objective account, because what we observed and heard has been interpreted and represented. In a similar vein, we would acknowledge both the impact of the observer on the setting – an effect we sought to minimise and to make due allowance for. Our fieldworker's age and gender, obviously, were highly significant to the conduct of the research. The outcome, as will be evident and is probably inevitable, is that we gathered more extensive data on some households than others.

A frequent concern was the impact of the researcher on the setting: some research subjects in particular seemed to almost feel obliged to engage in some form of media consumption for the benefit of the researcher. Others ceased using media to talk with us. It was sometimes hard to judge what was normal behaviour, as routines are interrupted by more spontaneous actions. Nonetheless, what we have done is to make sense of our data in a way that lets it speak. At the same time, what we have written is a fiction, it is something that we have made up,[83] so in this sense our account is contestable.

While rejecting notions of naturalism, our analysis has been informed, first and foremost, by what we heard and saw. We analysed the fieldwork data in terms of what emerged. At the same time, and inevitably, we drew on our prior interests and expertise (for example, in relation to new media technologies). We also focused on some important issues and concepts that have been developed by other qualitative researchers of media users; and the media organisations involved in the project had alerted us to some particular interests or concerns (for example, uses of EPGs, and issues concerning the language). On this basis we generated the categories that we used to analyse, structure and write about what we observed and heard.

Finally, we undertook a little respondent validation – returning to the field to discuss with our informants what we had written about them. This was one important way of checking the validity of what we had written. Their responses are summarised below.

Reflexivity is a crucial part of ethnographic research. We conclude this account of our research methods, and bring it and the fieldwork 'to life', by providing as a coda the brief reflections by our fieldworker on his fieldwork in each household. Each concludes with a short paragraph on how members of the household responded to the cameo we had written about them (in Chapter 2 of this book).

Addey and Rowlands (Swansea)

The advantage and disadvantage of working with Paul Addey and Christopher

83   Clifford Geertz (1988) *Works and Lives: The Anthropologist as Author*, Cambridge, Polity.

Rowlands was that both are the same age as I am, of a similar social and cultural background, and share my interests and tastes – for example, in music, film, computer games and performing in bands. In many respects they reflect my student lifestyle prior to my marriage and becoming a parent – making the household one of the most comfortable to work in, but also one of the most difficult. Things appeared so natural that it was difficult to make the familiar strange, a process that would be easier in a less familiar setting.

Access to the household was dependent on my being accepted by the lads and having something in common. Shared tastes facilitated discussion of music and film, and speaking Welsh was useful, given their mission to learn the language.

The only strain was that I could participate in household activities only to a certain degree. For example, when playing console games with the group of friends while they were also drinking alcohol, I had to calculate my actions to maintain – although not communicate to others – the role of researcher.

In many respects, this household represents in microcosm the problem of the researcher–subject relationship. What I decided was to join in with the activities of the household to the fullest. In some respects this was going native, no longer a researcher, but a guest enjoying the company and hospitality of the household. I made fieldnotes back at home, after the fieldwork, when I could reflect on the experience and make the familiar strange again.

The problem of going native was overcome by acting in one way while thinking in another. In this household I played the role of the lad rather than the researcher, but always maintained an internal self that was focused on the research.

The lads thought that they had been represented fairly in their cameo, though they felt that we had made much of their late-night drinking and gaming and not much else. Paul reflected with humour that his life was sad and that the research had made him seem like a lonely old alcoholic. They feel that the problems they faced as Welsh learners had been expressed clearly and commented that they had enjoyed taking part in the project and felt that they had contributed to something worthwhile.

Chandler and Thomas (Carmarthen)

The subjects have different interests but are about my age, which in many respects presupposes a degree of commonality. At first, they were intrigued to know how someone of college-leaving age had a research position. Stuart has recently graduated and spoke in depth about his frustration at gaining only a clerical post and his aspirations to get on. He and I spent some time in the pub talking about the nature and difficulties of fieldwork in households, and Stuart was keen to stress his awareness of the effect of the researcher on the research environment. We spent a considerable time going into the aims of the research. In this sense, my time in Carmarthen was the most open and honest in terms of our aims.

Stuart seemed to want to be informed in considerable detail. He had an interest in the project and wanted the opportunity to validate our observations and analysis, which almost seemed a condition of his continuing participation. After time in their house taking notes, Stuart would join me for a drink to discuss what I had just observed, to comment on relevant issues and to respond to questions.

I did not have the chance to get to know Ann as well as I did Stuart. The three of us spoke at their home quite easily, but she often left me in Stuart's company, and always declined invitations to join us for a drink. She made me feel welcome, but sometimes left the two of us alone to go upstairs to watch television on her own. In other words, there was a profoundly gendered dimension to my relationship with these two.

Stuart seemed to want the research process to be a two-way flow: he in particular liked to find out as much about me as I wanted to know about them. In principle this is true of all our households. Reciprocity and gestures of hospitality demand that researchers reveal a great deal about themselves, their backgrounds, values and tastes. This is an integral part of the ongoing negotiation of access and of the maintenance of effective fieldwork relations.

Ann told Stuart that the cameo shows that he does nothing round the house. Stuart told me that he did not realise the house was split between them – with the television upstairs for her and Sky downstairs. They laughed at the description of the house as seeming different from their style, which they thought was a bit cheeky. Apart from this, they felt that they came across very well and seemed pleased that something of their lives might contribute to a research study. Stuart told me, tongue in his cheek, that "it's nice to be special, isn't it", although I held the feeling that this was nearer to the truth than he might like to admit.

Daniels (Ammanford)

Doing fieldwork with the Daniels was easy and difficult in equal measure. Mrs Daniels made me feel completely at home and at ease, while Mr Daniels made me feel quite the opposite. It was difficult to get time to talk with him because of his busy routine and when we did, he did not like me using a tape recorder.

Writing notes only intruded further, but over time Mr Daniels provided some of our richest data. He was particularly honest and forthright, and I got the idea that my presence had little impact on his behaviour, which was good. After getting to know Mr Daniels I found him an intelligent and witty man – an interesting conversationalist with a broad general knowledge.

During the early stages of fieldwork, I spent a considerable time mucking out stables with Mrs Daniels and generally trying to make my presence useful. This work paid off, as I was allowed to eat with the family at weekends, like other workers and friends. These times were most fruitful in terms of observations (and I learned something about horses, too). Unlike some households, my presence was tolerated only if I did not get in the way and if I contributed to the activities going on around me. They were a pragmatic and busy business and agricultural family, and did not have time for those who did not make an effort to show their worth.

It was difficult to spend time in the living room, because it was so dominated by Mr Daniels. Most of my observations of this room were from the adjoining dining room, or from the accounts of other family members. Relations with the oldest son was helped by my taking an interest in motorcycles and rock music – which improved our interaction and brought down the barriers between researcher and respondent. The Daniels' home, like some of the others, came to be an open house, and its members became friends. This allowed me to get the richness of detail that makes the Daniels one of the most absorbing households in the study.

Mr Daniels did not like the way he had been portrayed as a tyrant in his own home and felt that the description of him had captured only his rest times and that at other times he was lively and dynamic. The rest of the family thought that it was funny. Mrs Daniels liked the fact that she was portrayed as the linchpin of the household and that her activities had been noted – if only to show Mr Daniels how lazy he was around the house. She felt that their household seemed quite unique when presented in writing, though she acknowledged that they were really far from typical or ordinary. She noted that the house was described as cluttered, and asked in jest, "do you mean messy then?"

Davies (Canton, Cardiff)

This household was the most challenging in terms of negotiating access. Initial contact was through a friend of Nicola's, whom I knew in my last job. It became apparent, however, that using friends and acquaintances to make contacts on my behalf could be a long and unpredictable process. The time she took to respond with any news was long and frustrating. Her first response was to be unsure of the motives of the research and unwilling to meet me without another person present. Finally a meeting was arranged, only to find that she no longer wanted to participate, as my presence in the household would make her relationship with her partner more strained.

Difficulties negotiating access elsewhere led me to ask her friend to try once again. In the interim, Nicola and her partner had separated, so I had the opportunity to meet with her and our mutual friend. Nicola and I being a similar age and different gender was a distinct disadvantage. It seemed that she saw me as just another bloke, although being recently married and having a young daughter helped.

My major consideration at this stage was not to frighten Nicola away, so I needed to play each visit in a low-key and undemanding way. In this case, I decided not to state the amount of time we wanted to spend in the household but to hope that the first visit would go well enough to facilitate another. Details of her use of the media had to be extracted from the conversations that took place in my presence, rather than me leading the discussions at this early stage in the research as I had in other households. With Nicola, questions were directed in a less formal manner.

This flexible and relaxed approach worked well in that I gained her trust to some degree. She was friendly and open, but concerned over the effect of my presence on her personal relationships. I decided that our next meeting would be best in her parents' house, after which I might move to a stage where I could participate and observe her and the daughter in their household. However, given her insecurity about my role as a researcher, my age, and so on, undertaking fieldwork and getting her to see me as a researcher were not easy.

For later visits I decided to appear more professional or academic, particularly when Nicola and I might be alone. Leaving a research diary went some way to giving the right sort of impression, but developing a relationship with Nicola was harder than in other households. Although I normally found some common ground with our research subjects, I felt it was better to remain more detached with Nicola. The research ended with me not really getting to know her as I would have liked, although amazed at the access that I managed to achieve given the circumstances.

Nicola was concerned that readers would view her as tied to her parents' apron strings. She felt that her independence and achievements were somewhat overshadowed by our portrayal of her close relationship with her parents. She felt that this was normal, whereas we had represented it as something strange. She felt that she seemed a lot younger in the cameo than in real life and saw this as the result of single mothers being stereotyped as young and financially dependent on the state. She appreciated that we had written something about her strong will to get a job and to make their home nice and comfortable.

James (Bangor)

The James' busy lifestyle and remote location do not really lend themselves to the casual visitor or ethnographer. Each member of the family led a busy life, so time was precious to them as individuals and time together as a family was also valued – so I felt honoured to enjoy access to their private lives. The household was unusual, in that its members were rarely together in the house at the same time. They were, however, keen for me to visit when they were all there. So I felt that I rather missed out on their more private or fragmented uses of the media. They had participated in a research project before, about local history, and felt at ease with me because of this. Indeed, from the outset they were eager to co-operate because they had enjoyed the previous experience.

Their busy lifestyle meant considerable ongoing negotiation of access – it was necessary to take each visit as it came. Fieldwork in the James household showed the value of being up-front about the aims of the research and letting them know the level of commitment expected – the 30 hours of fieldwork that was our target. Unlike some other households, the logistics of travel and having to stay in Bangor made unarranged visits impossible, though they would have been valuable. Having said this, I was always made to feel extremely welcome, and was given hospitality and a bed for the night on several occasions.

As with other households, semi-structured interviewing changed to more integrated and casual visits. On one visit, they had bought baby clothes as a present for my daughter. One of the sons has spent some time with me and my family, staying over after competing in a local bike race. Having had contact with the family in a social capacity helped in developing the relationship. I still remain in contact with the boys and feel that I have made two good friends in north Wales.

The James felt that they had been represented in a good light, although Lucy was shocked at how outspoken she seemed on moral issues. Also she did not realise the extent to which she had a regular pattern of television and newspaper use. They seemed surprised that I had described the house as so grand, stressing that it was no mansion or stately home. They all liked the pseudonyms that we chose for them and found these amusing. They felt that they had been represented fairly and Lucy told me that she was glad that I had enjoyed my time there, and that they had enjoyed my visits too.

Lewis (Builth Wells, Powys)

The main issue about fieldwork in the Lewis household is the constraints on time imposed by a busy family. With young and older children, Karen Lewis finds every spare minute a bonus. She is a single mother and is quite protective of her children, screening those who might want to come into the household. The first major obstacle was finding a time to visit that suited the family. Karen works and the boys are both at school, with busy social lives. Karen was recently divorced, so family interaction and history had to be handled tactfully and sensitively.

Karen was reluctant for me to go there for fieldwork on particular days, usually if she had had a bad day at work. Often she later apologised, telling me "not to take any notice". Sometimes she indicated that she felt overwhelmed by her work and her household responsibilities. In such instances, I kept my visits short, or gave her the space that she needed. More delicately than in some other households, I had to judge the time to back off and when was a good time to call.

Getting the two sons interested in participating was also a great struggle. They needed to be convinced that I was not a schoolteacher (a context in which they had encountered my wife) and that my questions were not some kind of test. This was overcome by finding common ground with the lads in terms of computer gaming and sport – even buying the oldest a pint when I saw him out in the town. My style with the lads was quite informal, trying to be as cool as I could, but I still felt that they saw me as considerably out of touch with their interests. My approach was to not force issues. It was better to talk about their interests than about wider issues.

During the first visits, I noticed that it was Karen who forced the boys to participate, somewhat against their will. Rhodri, the younger, was particularly quiet, while Dafydd was more open. I decided it was therefore best to take my time with the lads, letting Rhodri open up in his own time. Over a short time, the boys felt that I was interested in them and that they could express opinions away from their mother. Karen also started to mellow from her initial arrangement of having the family together in one room for me to talk with them, with them facing me. This was not natural and did not work well, but things changed considerably, with the visits becoming less formal. Karen Lewis remains guarded about her family life and remains the strong moral guardian of the household, but she has allowed me in and to spend time with her sons, who provided some very rich data. I live quite near the family, so we often stop to talk on the street.

Karen told me that she was sure what we had written was fine, although she felt that the detail about her marriages was a bit personal. She felt it said much about her and the boys' lifestyle. Dafydd (the oldest) read it, laughed, and told me that he seemed like a slob in the cameo. His brother and sister did not read it. Karen seemed pleased that we had portrayed them as a close family with a strong commitment to the Welsh language. She liked the way she appeared as something of a superwoman, while insisting that she was not really.

Powell (Llandaf, Cardiff)

As one of the last households in which we started fieldwork, the Powells represented a unique challenge: how to go from complete strangers to in-depth fieldwork, with little time left for the research. We had taken a long time finding a suitable household (in terms of the sample we needed) willing to participate, and they seemed our last hope.

Brian and Rhian had two completely different approaches to my fieldwork in their home. Brian was prepared to allow me to see the family relaxed and natural, and was not afraid to show family life as it is. Rhian, however, like other mothers in the study, wanted to present the best image of the family at all times. She would turn the television volume down or switch it off when I arrived, and would sometimes switch to something more refined, rather than their usual programme choice. There was often disagreement between them about how they should present themselves. Getting behind their presentations of self was a problem.

The son, Gareth, seemed the most laid-back and natural. His routines and relationship with his parents were quite enjoyable to witness, as he seemed as much of an observer of them as I was. He played the role of the teenage son perfectly, with his disassociation from his family, and his use of his bedroom as his sanctuary from us all.

There was a sense in the household that there were boundaries that I was not allowed to cross and aspects of family life that I should not see. I found it difficult to establish common ground that would facilitate a more open relationship, although they were happy for me to visit. They were willing to participate, I felt, because they felt flattered to be subjects, representing – as they saw themselves – the upwardly mobile, modern elite of Wales. However, there seemed a distance kept, particularly by the mother, with me as the researcher.

Like any visitor, the novelty of being in the household began to wear off, particularly after a three-day stint with the family. I learnt when to back off, because their willingness to participate in the project had definite time limits.

Brian felt that he had been described in a way that made it seem that his wife did all the work and that all he did was sit around watching television or playing golf. Gareth felt his father had portrayed him as a troublesome teenager. They were amused by the description of their collective use of the television – because, they said, this is such a rare occurrence. Rhian seemed amused to have come out of the report as the strong player – in their choice of films, for example – and had not realised how little time she has to herself and to read the newspaper and watch television.

Protheroe (Colwinston, Vale of Glamorgan)

The main challenge with the family was that they spend much of the year in France, so I had to try to maximise my visits in the short time they were at home. The family was the most welcoming, and treated me really well. They provided a bed for the night and evening meals during my visits. In return, I helped Angharad in the garden. Angharad, like others, consistently emphasised that they were not television addicts, so during my visits the television was put on only occasionally. Their grandchildren spend a lot of time with them and they tended to open up the household to the research. The Protheroes were at their most natural during the grandchildren's visits and the children provided comments and insights into the family's lifestyle.

At one time they asked me whether I was related to someone they had known, as my surname was unusual. I had never met the Protheroes before the research, but it turned out that they had been friends of my great uncle in Morriston. Amazingly, during my overnight stay in the house, I was given a room that contained some items of furniture made by my family many years ago. This link was rewarding for me, but it also gave me a connection with the family, which led to more flexible access.

There was one particular time in the household that I felt that the research would be derailed. This was due to the interest of their daughter and family in the research. They spend a considerable amount of time with Geoff and Angharad and I felt that they were more interested in the research than were Geoff and Angharad. There was a real danger that I would be pulled away from my original household and towards a new one, and a new set of household dynamics. Essentially, the more they wanted to speak to me, the less I managed to speak with Geoff and Angharad. It was a case of the whole family wanting to have their say and showing a genuine interest in communicating their feelings and opinions. This was resolved by explaining the household types that the research aimed to cover and politely saying 'thanks, but no thanks'.

The household is one of the more affluent in our sample, so their lifestyle contrasted well with some of our other households – although they always stressed that they had worked for what they have. Geoff's parents, unlike Angharad, are from quite a working class area of Swansea and I found them very modest about their obviously comfortable lifestyle. The Protheroe's were particularly kind and hospitable people and always made me feel almost like one of the family.

The couple read through their cameo very briefly and said that it seemed fine. They told me politely that they would be glad to be help anytime. They seemed pleased to be represented as loyal *Western Mail* readers and wanted the paper to know about its readers – they thought that this flow of information could not be a bad thing for improving the newspaper's appeal. They seemed positive that the newspaper had an interest in its readership.

Riley (Wrexham)

Richard Riley made it quite clear from the start, in his usual jovial manner, that I was allowed to visit during the day only because he likes to have company since he retired. This accounted for Richard's time, openness, and indeed patience with all my questions. He seemed happy to spend time talking and going about his business with me there. He seemed glad to have someone to converse with and to show me his handiwork in the shed, the garden, and even his skills in the kitchen. I spent most of my time in the household in Richard's company. I would liked to have spent more with his wife, but she has a far busier schedule than he does. Our shared love of music made talking to Richard fun, although he often lost me with his knowledge of jazz and classical music – which he found amusing and which seemed to make him feel as if he had something to teach me.

The most frustrating part of the research with the Rileys was my impact. For example, I once turned up and knocked on the back door. Through the door I could see the two of them reading the newspaper, but on my arrival the newspapers would be put down and we would begin to talk. They tended to see every chat as an interview, which made observation and note-taking more difficult. In the living room, the Rileys watched television or listened to music, but it was very difficult to judge if these were normal circumstances or in some way staged, although there did not seem to be an unnatural atmosphere. The main limitation was my lack of time with the household. The Rileys were the last household to come on board, so I had the least amount of time to get to know them. I felt that there was a lot more to learn about this household. They were friendly and very kind and we got on quite well, but I needed to push quite hard to get to the stage of being able to find out anything substantial about the Rileys.

I'm left with the feeling that I might have pushed them harder for access, but believe that this might have frightened them away altogether.

The Rileys felt that their lives were reminiscent of a sitcom, something like *One Foot in the Grave* – with him staying about the house causing mischief while she does all the work. They told me that it was strange to read someone else's 'take' on their everyday lives and, while they thought it had captured a snapshot of certain aspects of their lives, the cameo represented little more in reality. They said that it was like reading caricatures of themselves. They enjoyed reading it and found nothing that offended them.

Swaine (Merthyr Tydfil)

The first thing I noticed when negotiating access to the Swaine household was that they were very compliant and willing to participate. My first meeting with Michelle went very well, although she seemed nervous and not at all herself. The title of our research project and the name of The Open University had opened the door, but they also made her feel that this was going to be an inquisition. By the end of the first visit I felt that the children had taken to me, and thus I had passed the first test. Negotiation of further access was crucially dependent on getting on with the children.

The most difficult aspect of working in this household, but also the most rewarding in terms of access, were the children. Their demanding and inquisitive nature meant that, as a researcher, I could not hide behind a notebook or quietly observe in the corner. When I attempted to make notes as events occurred, the children sometimes came over, looked over my shoulder and read out what was on the page. When I used the tape recorder the children became intrigued by the microphone. Christopher spoke directly into it, while Amy started to sing and tap dance – and thus the interview was terminated. I was on their turf, they had a natural curiosity towards me, and I had to engage with them. I spent a great deal of time playing Nintendo and pool with the children – as Michelle said, "otherwise they'll never leave you alone". So to spend any time in the household, I had to devote considerable energy to interacting with the children. A few hours in the household felt like a week. Michelle often joked that this would put me off having children. Because John worked shifts, my presence allowed Michelle to cook or to converse with me. It was vital that I played with the children, or Michelle found it too demanding to have us all in the house at the same time.

The children meant that the household was incredibly busy, so I felt that there was little pretence, front, or conscious self-presentation on the part of the family: what you saw was what it was. The family simply got on with things, regardless of whether I was there or not. They often said things like "don't mind the mess" or "I'm sorry about the noise". The experience seemed authentic, and was certainly interesting.

The children were really interested in our video and sound recording equipment. I felt that I should give the family the use of the video camera for a week, as they did not own one. They seemed grateful for this and used it to film the children and kept this on video cassette. This acted as a great means to cement my relations with the children and adults and paved the way for unlimited access to the household, on a pop-around basis.

The Swaines laughed at how their children's activities had been captured in print. They felt that they watched a lot of television and agreed that the television was a babysitter for them. Michelle felt that we had portrayed them as anti-Welsh and stressed that they were not – while John remained unchanged in his view on this. They felt that the cameo said a lot about their lifestyle and family routines and were glad that they had been anonymised in the research, as Michelle felt that much of the content was personal. She appreciated, however, that our work was concerned to portray real people.